D1267880

WILL

YOU

GO?

WILL YOU GO?

A Journey *to* Emotional *and* Spiritual Freedom

MELONY MATERI

39999000033390

Little Elm Public Library
Little Elm, TX 75068

WITHDRAWN

Will You Go?
© 2017 by Melony Materi

All rights reserved.

Unless otherwise marked, all Scriptures are taken from The Holy Bible,
New International Version®, NIV® Copyright ©1973, 1978, 1984, 2011
by Biblica, Inc.® Used by permission. All rights reserved worldwide.

Scriptures marked NKJV are taken from the New King James Version®.
Copyright © 1982 by Thomas Nelson. Used by permission. All rights reserved.

Scriptures marked NABRE are taken from the New American Bible,
revised edition © 2010, 1991, 1986, 1970 Confraternity of Christian Doctrine, Inc.,
Washington, DC All Rights Reserved. No part of this work may be reproduced
or transmitted in any form or by any means, electronic or mechanical, including
photocopying, recording, or by any information storage and retrieval system,
without permission in writing from the copyright owner.

Scripture quotations marked MSG are taken from *The Message*.
Copyright © 1993, 1994, 1995, 1996, 2000, 2001, 2002.
Used by permission of NavPress Publishing Group.

To protect the privacy of certain individuals,
the names and identifying details have been changed.

ISBN: 978-0-9959978-0-6 (printed)
ISBN: 978-0-995 9978-1-3 (ebook)

Cover design: Jeff Gifford: gradientidea.com
Editor: Vanessa Carroll: vanessacarroll.wordpress.com
Interior design: Beth Shagene: page-turnerdesign.com
Proofread: Allyson Swan

Printed in the United States of America

First printing in 2017

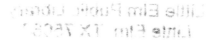

To my grandsons:
Austin, Alex, and Ronan,
I love you.
This book is for you, your children,
and your children's children.

CONTENTS

As for me, I will always have hope;
I will praise you more and more.
My mouth will tell of your righteous deeds,
of your saving acts all day long—
though I know not how to relate them all.
I will come and proclaim your mighty acts, Sovereign LORD;
I will proclaim your righteous deeds, yours alone.
Since my youth, God, you have taught me,
and to this day I declare your marvelous deeds.
Even when I am old and gray,
do not forsake me, my God,
till I declare your power to the next generation,
your mighty acts to all who are to come.
Your righteousness, God, reaches to the heavens,
you who have done great things.
Who is like you, God?
Though you have made me see troubles,
many and bitter,
you will restore my life again;
from the depth of the earth
you will again bring me up.
You will increase my honor
and comfort me once more.

PSALM 71:14–21

PREFACE

"Come and work for me . . ." I listened again. Was I hearing things? I had been spending time every morning in prayer, but this was different. Opening my eyes, I tried to reassure myself that the voice I heard in my heart was real and closed them again. I had a vision. On the edge of a cliff, I looked into a deep dark abyss. Jesus was there, beckoning, His voice almost audible. He said the words again. "Come and work for me . . ."

I laugh, thinking back to my response. Lifting my hands in the air, I looked up and exclaimed, "But You don't pay anything!"

I took pride in my career as a Rural Municipal Administrator; a nice name for a property tax collector. It had been part of my identity for over twenty years. I made a decent amount of money. I was good at it. I had to be. I paid a heavy price for it. I was not about to give it up because Christ, Himself, asked me.

But the vision and His words plagued me.

I had told my husband Lawrence that I felt God asking me to quit my job.

"You will never quit your job, Melony," he scoffed, "It's too important to you." I told him about the vision, but he had made the same statement.

There was another reason it would've been foolish to resign at that time. A few months earlier I had been diagnosed with the dreaded "C" word—cancer. We sat at the kitchen table, tears flowing. How could this be happening? How could God do this? Surgery was scheduled to remove a portion of my thyroid. The call would come at any time.

But thoughts of the vision and Christ's words were unrelenting. Christ was like a head hunter who searched for someone to fill a particular position. I did everything possible to avoid applying.

But I was being set up—even pushed.

A month later, I walked into the house after work. Lawrence sat in his chair in the living room, reading a book.

"How was your day?" he asked.

"Fantastic! I quit my job today. I gave one month's notice."

His mouth dropped. His book dropped.

April 16, 2007 was my last day. How would I make a living? Surgery was scheduled for a few weeks. People thought me crazy to be quitting. For months afterward, they asked if I missed my job. I never have. The freedom I felt closing the office door was unmistakable. The chains broke.

Three weeks later, things were not going as planned. Home from the surgery, I wasn't feeling great. My temperature was elevated, and the wound on my throat turned red—a sure sign of infection. Lawrence rushed me to Emergency. The doctor phoned the surgeon, asking what procedure to follow. She was to remove the stitches and reopen the wound to allow the infection to seep out. I was admitted into the hospital for the week with a regimen of strong antibiotics. When you have a large open wound, you can't just put a Band-Aid on it and expect it to heal. Every day, eighteen feet of quarter inch packing was removed from the wound. It was cleaned, drained, and the packing replaced. At home, nurses came daily to repeat the process. Five weeks later, the wound was small enough for a Band-Aid.

Sometimes you learn you are not the one in control. This was one of those times. A few weeks later, they determined there had been a slight mistake. The wrong side of the thyroid had been removed. To say I was stunned would be putting it mildly.

Everyone thought I should sue, but I called the surgeon and forgave him. More biopsies were taken. The cancer was gone, a miracle?

Why did God allow this to happen? To this day, I use it as an analogy for emotional pain. We all have pain. We all try to go over, under, or around it. We all do things to ease the pain, to numb it, to anesthetise it. We all try to use Band-Aids to cover up our pain, but the infection will only spread even though we think it's under control, but for emotional pain, there is only one cure—emotional surgery. You must go back to the wound and reopen it. The infection must be let out. It must be cleaned, drained, and repacked with the word of God until all that's left is a scar. Healing must take place from the inside out.

LIFE LESSON #1: Trying to avoid emotional pain will only cause bitterness and resentment. It will infect not just you, but those around you.

I had done what God had asked. I had quit my job. Now what?

**Little Elm Public Library
Little Elm, TX 75068**

PART I

In the Beginning

CHAPTER 1

Before adopting me, my parents were my foster parents. They had a natural son, then adopted a son, then had a natural daughter, then adopted me.

Two different couples took me home, only to bring me back because I didn't "fit in." The threads of a cocoon of shame began knitting themselves together. Later, Dad told me that Mom had said with exasperation, "Why on earth don't they want her? This is just crazy!" The die was cast. They kept me. But, they did not understand that when adopting a child, a wounded soul was being brought into their home, someone who would test their patience and limits.

Sexual abuse started at a young age, by someone close. The memories were vivid; I thought I must've been seven or eight years old. But that was not the case. I was much younger. The cocoon of shame began to cover me.

I cried out for help the only way many children know how—wetting the bed past the age of most children, stealing, and playing with matches. Mesmerised, I watched the spark ignite the small but explosive fire on the end of the small stick, not caring whether I left burn marks anywhere. Mom caught me one day and sent me to my room. She had no idea the burn marks were a huge SOS sign to her in the sand of my spirit. She came to my room with a stick. She kept hitting me, insisting a friend must have been there as I lit the matches. I cried and wailed, "Please stop! No one was with me!" But the hitting continued until I gave her the name of a friend down the street. I will never forget how that felt. What had I done? It was the only way to get her to stop. I wish I would have allowed the hitting to continue. It would have been far better than the sickening sensation that followed.

I had no understanding yet of how her own emotional traumas had affected her. That, mixed with now knowing that adoptees can have misplaced emotions in the relationships with their adoptive mothers, meant it was not easy for either of us. Mom and Dad had no way of knowing the rejection and abandonment issues that can come with an adopted child.

At ten years of age, we moved from Calgary and took over the family farm in the neighbouring province of Saskatchewan.

We seemed comfortable there. Dad worked off-and-on on the farm.

I made friends at school and had what I thought a normal childhood.

One night I had a dream. I dreamt I walked on a path. It was a dry, arid, sandy place. A man walked beside me, he wore white. I felt a profound sense of security and peace with Him. I knew the man was Jesus Christ. I told no one about the dream.

We attended a church until I was six years old. Dad had been having financial problems and could not pay tithes to the church for a time. So the elders decided, in their wisdom, to pay a visit to Mom and Dad. The elders said if they were unable to pay their tithes, it was not suitable to bring their children to Sunday school. That ended my relationship with the church as a child. When we moved to the farm, mom did everything possible to drag me to church, one morning literally pulling my body out of bed. But why would I want to go? That was where *those* people were. It was Mom's last-ditch attempt to bring me under control. If she couldn't do it, maybe God could. But the writing was on the wall.

At the time, Dad could not forgive what the elders had said and was unable to come to a place of knowing life lesson number two.

Dad was a strong, gentle man, and a good listener who disciplined only when necessary. If he disciplined, we deserved it.

At the age of eight, while still living in the city, one of my
brothers tattled on me. I stole a package of cigarettes from the
store and he saw my friends and me smoking. He pedaled home
as fast as possible to tell Dad.

When I arrived home, I was sent to my room to await a
spanking. Dad's hands were as big as baseball mitts. But the
waiting was worse than the punishment.

The next day, we went to the zoo. It was as though he had
totally forgotten what I had done. There is no doubt he played a
huge role in my life, helping me learn how to receive and understand the mercy of God.

After moving to the farm, I remember a time when all of us
kids were playing outside. I was bugging my brothers and sister,
so they kept saying Dad was calling me from the house. They
were just trying to get rid of me, but I thought I'd better check.
Dad was in the basement, I called out to him, "Dad? Dad, do you
want me?"

He stood at the bottom of the stairs. "What kind of question
is that? Of course, I want you. I will always want you!"

I have never forgotten that. I never felt more loved.

But the maker of the cocoon of shame continued to weave
threads around me. Another incident happened at the age of ten.
We lived a mile from a small village, population eighty, counting the cats and dogs. I rode my bike in to play with a friend.
On my way home, a short distance away from the farm, I saw a
dirty, white older car on the corner that wasn't moving. A man
wearing camouflage clothing, who had straggly, shoulder length,

blonde hair sat in the driver's seat. As I rode closer, he rolled down his window. He kept asking me to show him something. "Show me your pussy," he demanded.

I kept looking toward the farm and said, "I'm sorry, I don't understand what you're asking." I was a naive ten-year-old girl.

He said it again.

"They're back at the farm. I can take you there," I said hesitantly. His frustration levels rose.

"Pull your pants down!" he yelled, and I froze. He started getting out of the car and I pedaled as fast as my legs would go . . . to safety . . . to security, until there were no cars in sight.

I shudder, thinking of what could've happened. God protected me that day. I never spoke a word to anyone. Later, it would be used as one of the best examples in my life of how a "trigger" works.

CHAPTER 2

After we took over the family farm, I had asthma attacks, bad enough at times that I wished I was dead. But that wasn't the only problem. I had unidentifiable attacks of pain around my heart. I was taken to various doctors and they could not figure what was wrong. At times, the pain was so severe, my movements were paralyzed. It would last seconds to minutes. I stood or sat motionless and breathed shallowly until it subsided. Later in my life, after removing the emotional Band-Aids I had been using, the "heart pain" mysteriously disappeared.

Shortly after I turned fifteen, my family attended a function for the person who had sexually abused me. I was to attend also, but it took place during some school final exams. Of course, with typical behavior of someone who has been abused, I had never told Mom and Dad. I convinced them that I would be okay on the farm. They drove out of the farmyard.

Alone, I opened the cupboard door to the liquor and poured a glass of whiskey. The taste on my lips and in my mouth was bitter as I swallowed hard and choked down the liquid courage. I lost count as one ounce led to another. I never heard the phone ringing as Mom and Dad tried frantically to call. I was passed out, naked in the bathtub in my own vomit—another SOS sign in the sand that no one saw. My aunt and uncle were sent to find out what was happening. They cleaned me up and took me to their home. I sat the next day writing an exam. My hands shook, and I couldn't think straight. Not a word was said about the incident. It would be years before I realized that even then, I had not dealt with the abuse. The cocoon tightened.

The previous summer, I started dating. A boy took an interest in me. I didn't notice Mom's nervousness, until one day, Dad drove her to the psych ward. She was admitted and spent a few months there. Her psychiatrist asked Dad and I to come in for an appointment. I felt important in a weird way.

Then came the clincher. The psychiatrist said I was the reason for Mom's nervous breakdown, she worried I would become pregnant. He did not connect this with her eight miscarriages and stillborn child. She never faced the emotional pain birthed with those traumatic events; they gave her shock treatments instead. But her nervous breakdown was deemed my fault; I was responsible for her pain.

Years later, Dad brought the memory back up again. Even then, I hung my head, recalling the incident. But Dad had other thoughts. He said, "I should've reached across that psychiatrist's desk and punched his lights out."

But the cocoon of shame had already continued to wrap itself around me, its maker delighting in how it was taking shape.

LIFE LESSON #3: Wisdom and knowledge are not the same.
Wisdom does not come with education.

Little did Mom know, her worries were prophetic. And little did Mom or Dad realize that it is not uncommon for an adoptee to have an unplanned pregnancy. Little did I realize, I would do anything to keep from being abandoned by my boyfriend. That included giving away the one thing God considered a gift to be given to my future husband. But because of things that happened, I didn't view virginity as being very important.

Within a few months, I missed my period. As the weeks ticked by, I hoped beyond hope it would come, but unlike my period, the days just kept flowing. My boyfriend and I did something stupid, but it seemed a good idea at the time. We both took the money out of our savings accounts—$380. I was fifteen years old and he seventeen, when we ran away from home.

LIFE LESSON #4: Running away from something doesn't make it go away.

We came up with a plan. We drove to the nearest city to get a hotel room for me for the night, and then he returned home with his parent's vehicle to get his motorcycle. I took a bus to another city in the north the next morning. We were to meet there, get jobs and make something of ourselves. After the baby's birth, we would come back, all grown up. That was the plan, simple. right?

The bus pulled into the station with him nowhere in sight. I waited, and I waited, and I waited. Hours went by. A mixture of dread and panic filled me. Had I been abandoned? My heart held its breath.

I could hear the motor of another bus. He appeared. The motorcycle broke down and someone gave him a ride to the nearest town where he caught the next bus.

For two weeks, no one knew our whereabouts. Money was running out paying for the hotel room, so we rented an apartment. When we were on the street and saw a police car, we hid. Dale got a job as a vacuum cleaner salesman. I tried to get a job as a waitress, but no one was interested in hiring a fifteen-year-old. Within two weeks, we knew it would not work so we called home. The next day, our parents came to see us. Of course, they wanted to know why we ran away from home, but we did not divulge our secret. We said we did not want to come home. No doubt they thought that if forced, we would run again. We were allowed to stay and try to make a go of it.

Within weeks, I could feel my body changing.

I could no longer hide the growing secret. With my heart racing and nerves numb, I told Mom while in the waiting room to see her psychiatrist. It seemed a safe place to tell her. She wasn't agitated, but when we got home and told Dad, she started making plans for me to terminate. No one would ever have to know . . .

But I could already sense this tiny being in my body. Even now as I rewind and look at that moment, it's hard to put into words how I was affected when she tried pushing abortion on me. As someone who was adopted, I was clearly "unplanned." Deep in my heart, I felt I was a mistake. Is that what people do with mistakes? Either abort or place for adoption? Mom adopted me, yet wanted me to abort. What was left of my self-esteem went into the toilet. The cocoon of shame was almost complete.

I couldn't do it. I couldn't abort. Adoption seemed like the next best thing. I moved back home.

The principal did not allow me to go to school. Lessons were dropped off for subjects and the rest were taken by correspondence. I took good care of myself and went into nurture mode. If there was one thing I could give this child, it was good health.

Dad took me to doctor's appointments in the small city

thirty miles away. During one appointment, my water broke—right there in the examination room. Dad drove to the hospital. It stormed that night, both outside the hospital and inside my heart. My boyfriend, Dale, picked up Mom. After a short stay, Dad decided they should go home. He recognized that Dale and I needed to do this on our own. Within five hours, our first daughter was born. Only someone who has given birth would understand—this being you have been connected with for nine months, this being that knows whether you like onions or pumpkin pie, this being that knows whether you prefer rock or classical or country, this being that knows the essence of your voice, this being that has relied on your every breath to stay alive. Within moments, the pain of childbirth was gone. The nurses showed her to me and then took her away. The physical pain left, but the emotional pain started.

Dale left for home for a while. I was alone. And my daughter Jodie was alone. My heart ached.

I wandered to the nursery to gaze at her. My family came to see her. I rolled her bassinet into the room. Was I doing the right thing? No one prepared me for the emotions that bombarded me. It was like a final exam in school that I didn't study for. But this was not a test in school. This was my daughter and one of the most extreme emotional tests I would ever face.

Instead of leaving the hospital with my daughter in my arms, I left the hospital with the bouquet of red roses from Mom and Dad. No one mentioned her. We were to just move on. When they took her away, my heart went with her. I numbed, trying to put on a front.

Ten days after giving birth, I could no longer keep shoring up the emotional dam. I kept trying to plug the leaks, but there were too many. Pillows were wet with tears.

Dad then forever altered my life and that of my child. Sitting on the bed, he said, "If this is the way this will affect you, you better keep her."

I couldn't stand it any longer; I told Dale I wanted to get her. We picked up the absolute necessities and drove to the hospital. I called the social worker from there. She was upset, she had picked out people to be Jodie's parents. I told her I was sorry, but I was Jodie's mom . . . and I was taking her home. I was fifteen years old.

LIFE LESSON #5: *A baby doesn't know if you are single, married, rich, poor, a teenager, or a successful business person—all it knows is you are its mother.*

CHAPTER 3

Dale and I got engaged. But this life-altering decision needed the government's approval. Mom and Dad had to sign the marriage licence because I was not yet eighteen years old.

Astrology became important. Instead of putting faith in God, I put it into the occult. Dad and I went to see an astrologer together one day. My wedding day was fast approaching, so at the end of the session, I asked the astrologer whether I should get married. His answer dripped with wisdom and was one I would never forget. "If you must ask the question, you shouldn't be getting married."

We married. I was seventeen, Dale nineteen. We had already cheated on each other. I married with fingers crossed behind my back. But it seemed the right thing to do.

We bought a home, we were doing well. A business was for sale in our home town, so we bought it. It was a disaster.

I sat there watching television one day. What I did forever altered my world, my life, and my eternal life. The man said if I asked Jesus Christ into my life, He would be with me and would never forsake me. All my sins would wash away . . .

Things were not well. *What could this hurt?* I asked Him. There were no fireworks. Angels did not appear. But I knew that if this was the same Jesus from the dream when I was ten, I wanted to know Him. But it would be a long time before that would happen.

LIFE LESSON #6: *When you become a Christian, you must develop a relationship with Christ. You must seek Him.*

PART II

If You Do Not Maintain Your Relationship with Christ, Other Gods Will Start to Appear

CHAPTER 4

We sold the business, but we didn't know how we would make ends meet. We both took menial jobs. A grade eleven education wasn't going very far. Working part time, I took subjects by correspondence and went back to the high school, taking classes with kids much younger. In my mind, my husband could not provide for our family. I had to do something. Did I trust God? No. I placed my trust in myself.

Taking off-campus university classes, I became a Rural Municipal Administrator—one of the main tasks being a property tax collector.

By this time, finances were improving. It was time for a "planned pregnancy."

I found a statistic one day. Sixty percent of people alive today were not "planned."

LIFE LESSON #7: Never tell someone they are a mistake. A child may not have been planned by his or her parents, but they were planned by God. And God does not make mistakes.

I will never forget the day Lindsey was born. After three hours of labor, she was laid on my stomach, seemingly unsure of what would happen next. "Well, hello there," I said softly. She arched her body, turning her head toward the voice she knew intimately. Our eyes met and locked. It was love at first sight. I was twenty-two years old.

By this time, I had completed the courses and classes necessary to be a municipal administrator. I was required to have one year of training with another administrator before taking a position in a municipal office. When Lindsey was three months old, I worked for no pay at a municipal office to gain the training required. Within a few months, a paid training position became available in the same small city where Dale worked, so we moved. Our marriage thrived. We were doing well. We loved each other.

That fall, after thirty-five years of marriage, my parents separated. People don't think a divorce affects adult children, but it does. Something broke, and there was nothing to fix it. The relationship between the two people who adopted me as one of their own shattered. Mom and Dad's relationship wasn't great, but it seemed solid—a foundation—a security and connection I could always count on. Part of me was ripped out with the divorce.

Within two months, the event that forever altered life took place. The pill wasn't a good method of birth control. When using it, I became a person I did not recognize. Instead, we used three different types of birth control in unison.

LIFE LESSON #8: *No matter what anyone tells you, there is only one way to avoid becoming pregnant, Abstinence.*

I sobbed as the same doctor who delivered Jodie and Lindsey into the world confirmed the pregnancy. "I can't possibly be pregnant now, not now . . ."

I had six months left in the training, which would enable me a position that paid well. Dale had just been demoted.

"This is just a blob of tissue, Melony. I can take care of your problem, and you will never have to worry about it again," my doctor promised.

LIFE LESSON #9: *If you don't make God the center of your life, Satan will show you other gods to worship.*

What was I going to do? Jodie was seven years old, Lindsey was ten months old. I had to take care of my family financially because Dale seemed unable. I went home and discussed it with him. He left the decision to me. Did I ask God for direction? No. Did I think God would answer me if I asked? No. Two weeks later, I aborted our third child.

I told my boss I needed to go into the hospital for tests that involved staying overnight. It was an extremely cold day. I was numb—physically, emotionally and spiritually. The counselling consisted of a nurse asking if I was sure this was what I wanted. It was the same hospital I initially walked out of without my first child. It was the same hospital I walked out of holding my second child. It was the same hospital I would walk out of after aborting my third child.

"Just breathe . . ." the anesthetist instructed, putting the mask over my mouth.

I breathed. In the last second before losing consciousness, I wanted to scream, "No!!!" But it was too late.

I awoke in the recovery room, crying and sobbing uncontrollably. A woman laid on a gurney, gazing at me as though I was from another planet. The nurse came over and patted my hand saying, "Don't worry Melony. Everything is going to be okay." But nothing was ever okay again.

When I look back now, Jesus was sitting there holding my hand. But He was crying far more than I was. He said He would never leave me and He hadn't. I left Him.

I walked out of the hospital without a bouquet of roses and without a child. It was official—money had become my god.

It was so cold I wondered if the car would start. I had driven thirty miles to the hospital, scared and alone. Dale stayed with Jodie and Lindsey while I stayed overnight to abort their sibling. *You had no choice,* I told myself. *You did what you had to do.* After a few attempts, the car roared to life.

I walked into the house and Dale hugged me. Emotions were barricaded into a room in my heart with a large "Do Not Enter" sign. I moved on, unaware of the cocoon of shame that continued to wrap itself around me, growing ever tighter, suffocating me.

I wrote a poem and buried it, hoping it would help me rid myself of the emotions that haunted me. It didn't.

Oh God, is it true what they say?
Am I damned for life eternally?
Will I never walk through Heaven's gates?
Is this my everlasting fate?

Have I deprived someone of their right to live?
Did I murder the life that dwelled in me?
Is the true battle against people such as I?
Is the price I must pay to continue to cry?

I'm not sure if I even believe in You,
I know that I once believed in myself,
But that belief is slowly starting to dwindle,
The light no longer am I able to kindle.

If people only knew the cost of my crime,
I can't stand to look at myself in the mirror,
I know that there's probably more to come,
A person filled with happiness, I'll never become.

They speak as though it was just another day,
They know not what they're talking about,
God, if for once they could stand in my place,
If my children knew, could they look in my face?

If it's true what they say about the sin I've made,
If it's true that I'll surely be cast into hell,
It doesn't matter to me if it was daughter or son,
This battle is over, Satan has won.

But emotions cannot be buried alive.

Within a few months, a municipal administrator's position opened. I was offered the job. We moved to a small town. The god of money wrapped a chain around me, locked it, and threw away the key.

LIFE LESSON #10: *When you try to avoid emotional pain in your life, you think you are in control of it, but it is controlling you.*

CHAPTER 5

No one ever told me about post-abortive grief, which can start within two years of an abortion. Drinking became a habit; I even did drugs once in a while. I became a dismissive parent, unaware that parents who have experienced abortions become either dismissive or over-protective. Every time I looked at my children, it was a subconscious reminder of the aborted child. My job became the number one priority. I had to be good at it. I had sacrificed a child on its altar. Subconsciously avoiding anything to do with babies became the norm—stores with baby clothing, people coming down the street with a stroller, baby showers.

I did not have friends. Are you kidding? They might find out about the deep, dark secret. I felt I was the only one in the world with a secret this big. Guilt and shame were my constant companions, masking themselves in various ways. I was a dead woman walking. But no one guessed, no one saw the mask.

Running even farther from God, I involved myself in numerology, Scientology, tarot cards, and psychics—anything but God. Why would He want me? One day, while attending a psychic fair in the city, I paid a man to read my head. A counsellor? No, this man could tell your fortune by feeling bumps on your head. I paid $75 for this illuminating service. Instead of putting faith in God, in the one who made the universe, the sun, the moon, the stars, the planets, the earth and all it contained, I put my faith in a man who read my head for $75.

Looking back, I wanted him to tell me the answer to the question of all questions—when would I die—when would I face God and pay for what I had done.

CHAPTER 6

Throughout life, I sensed a "calling." Unsure of what it was, I had a deep wish to sound the alarm, to blow the trumpet, but I had no clue how to play the notes.

After accepting an administrative position in a small town, a new pastor started at the church across the street from my office. I recognized his name from elementary school in Calgary. We met and talked of each other's life struggles.

At one point, he had wrestled with an addiction to drugs. I told him how proud I was of my brother who changed after a similar battle. The pastor talked of a group of kids at the Bible camp. The calling resonated. I asked him if he would like me to speak to them about abstinence. He loved the idea, and we made arrangements—the timeline a year and a half after one of my biggest secrets, the abortion.

It was a disaster. I talked of the pregnancy at age fifteen, but spoke nothing of the abortion. It would be years before sharing that it was the abortion that totally twisted my life, not the child

I had at fifteen. Within minutes of starting the "presentation," I sobbed uncontrollably, choking and sputtering while talking. It had no effect on the kids.

Still determined to speak about abstinence, I sent brochures to schools and churches in the area. How many replies did I receive? Zero. Zilch. None. God had a calling on my life, but it wasn't my time. He needed to do a great work in me before it was the right season.

LIFE LESSON #11: "There is a time for everything, and a season for every activity under the heavens." (Ecc. 3:1) You may believe it is the right time for something. But I suggest first asking the One in control of the seasons whether it is your time to bloom.

CHAPTER 7

Losing respect for Dale and for myself, I continued to sabotage my life. I became infatuated with a man named Lawrence and with his interest in me. With black hair and olive skin, he had the same physical characteristics as someone I would meet years later. He was a Catholic and of German descent.

We couldn't stay away from each other. I felt compelled to confess the abortion. Testing him, I was subconsciously asking *Do you still love me now?* I did not consider myself worthy, let alone lovable. Eventually the affair exposed itself. We told our spouses and tried to salvage the remnants of our marriages.

LIFE LESSON #12: If you do not think yourself worthy or lovable, you will do unworthy, unlovable things.

After this, I developed another longing that would not leave no matter how I tried to fill it, and so I started a search for my birth mother. I thought if I found her, the yearning would be filled that had haunted my whole life—to be complete and whole. The woman in me who had given birth needed to know the woman who had given birth to me.

It was 1989. There were no websites, email, or Facebook to search with. Knowing her surname and the potential place she lived, I sent letters to those in the area, the last line eerily saying, "I felt if I procrastinated any longer, it could jeopardize finding her." Mom and Dad never hid the adoption papers.

Nineteen years old when I was born, she was a fruit-packer, with siblings, a Ukrainian heritage, and high cheek bones. My birth father was a construction worker, with several siblings, of German descent, Catholic, with black hair and olive colored skin. But I was not interested in him.

One week later, the phone rang—one of *those* phone calls— the life altering kind. Dale answered the call from my birth mother's sister, a "birth aunt." My heart and mind raced as he handed me the phone.

They had received my letter. "*They*" were herself and her mother, my maternal grandmother. My birth aunt came home from work to find her mother sitting at the kitchen table, sobbing, with the letter clutched in her hand.

She said my mother's name was Pearl. My mind swirled. Where was Pearl? But my mind did not pick up on the tone in her voice when saying her name *was* Pearl.

"I'm so sorry to have to tell you this, Melony, but Pearl died six months ago."

"What?" I choked on the word. But there was more. She had gone missing for three months. A huge search was conducted, which ended when she was found frozen to death.

Tears of anticipation made way for tears of sorrow. She rambled on about my three half-brothers and two half-sisters.

That night, I slept fitfully, grieving the mother I would never meet. The next night, a half-sister called. Pearl told them about me before she died. And she left letters, some dated months earlier, some years earlier.

We made the trip to meet them the next week. It was strange to look like other people. One half-brother looked uncannily like the male version of me. We talked, laughed, and cried.

Someone handed me a file containing letters in my mother's handwriting. As I read, my heart opened and broke.

Dear Laura Lee,

I feel there is a need for me to write this letter to you. Twenty years have passed. I am the mother you never knew. I wake up and you are there. I feel bewildered, scared and confused at times. It seems like yesterday. Your hands were so small. I feel you may not understand why I surrendered you. You are always in my heart. I go to weddings and funerals and think about you. It's the way it is for me. You have brown hair and brown eyes. I see you everywhere. We are probably the same in many ways, but we probably will never know. It's twenty years later and I'm seeking information about you. I have to know. My children are grown now and I find it difficult to tell them about you. In time when I think it's right, I will. I lie awake at night and pray that everything will be okay for you. I hope you will forgive me and never forget me. When you bear your children, please think of me. I hope you think good thoughts about me. It would destroy me if you didn't. I had no help from your father or anyone. When I told my mother she was so upset. It was a nightmare. My parents said I couldn't stay home. They dropped me off in Calgary and I was alone. I was all alone. My life changed overnight. I remember the long days and nights. Time had no meaning for

*me. I prayed to God things would be okay for you and me. When
I signed the forms, I was never really the same. When they took
you from me I felt so guilty. Your brown eyes are there to see
and explore the world. If I live till I'm eighty, I will always see
those brown eyes watching me. I will always have this feeling of
rejection until time runs out for me. I have shed so many tears.
I have your picture. It stays in my heart. The final day I held
you I entered another world. I was empty. You were so beautiful. For seven days I held you to me. It was so cold, and I didn't
know what to do. I signed the papers, and I left for home. Love
is painful. I have loved you all my life. Birth, love and death
will always be there. Memories will live forever. I pray you have
been a happy child and that you try to find me. I hope we can
understand one another for it wouldn't be easy for a daughter
and mother to start from the beginning. I hope you will keep this
letter for it's all I have for now. I hope to live a long life for my
dream is to be friends. So I'm deceased before we meet, please
remember I always loved you Laura Lee.*

All I had to prove her existence were the letters, a blanket
she had knitted, and me. Emotions twisted and turned, evok-
ing thoughts of moving closer to my half-siblings at one point.
But the honeymoon feelings subsided. It wasn't them I had been
looking for . . .

> *For so long I sat and thought and wondered,*
> *Pondering on what I expected to find,*
> *Who you were and what you were like,*
> *Was I a past you wished left behind?*
>
> *A fear of rejection was always present,*
> *And I couldn't stand if that came true,*
> *Could it be that you had kept it a secret?*
> *Every birthday I had, I thought of you.*

I, too, almost gave my oldest girl away,
To more thoughts of you, this was a key,
With all I went through, I knew that somehow,
I wanted to find you and you wanted to find me.

Things happen for reasons that I don't understand,
Now I've come to realize my biggest fear,
I've found you and yet I never will find you,
Sorrow is the reason for all of my tears.

If only I could turn back the hands of time,
We'd meet and tears of joy I'd have cried,
In talking to your family, some comfort is found,
But I can't help feeling all the things I've been denied.

I wanted to feel so complete and whole,
Now all my dreams are shattered and blown,
I've never felt this kind of pain before,
You were looking for me, if only I'd known.

A thought formed. My very existence caused pain. I was the reason for my birth mother's pain. I was the reason for my adoptive mother's pain. It was my purpose in life.

Dale and I tried to glue the remnants of our shattered marriage, him willing to forgive everything that happened. But I did not want to be forgiven, for anything. We divorced.

Within three years of the abortion, I destroyed the family I believed I was saving. I successfully sabotaged our marriage. It became a statistic.

Lawrence's marriage did not survive, and we moved in together. Jodie was twelve, Lindsey five. His children no longer lived at home.

My heart rotted. Two marriages and two families destroyed. The cocoon completed, its maker hoping I would never emerge.

CHAPTER 8

We argued and fought. Someone said no matter what happened Lawrence would never marry me. I felt worthless and used. Needing to make myself "worth" something, I asked him if we would ever marry. The answer was *yes*. We surprised everyone by getting married by a Justice of the Peace. There. We were legitimate.

Did anything change? No. The fighting continued with me leaving many times, only to return. I destroyed the first marriage. I would not destroy another.

Lawrence wanted to return to church, but Christians were the last people I wanted to associate with. Once in a while he tuned in to a Christian radio station. I asked him to either shut it off or find another station. I wanted nothing to do with God.

Little did I know, God was pursuing me into my darkness.

CHAPTER 9

Years went by as I worked at the municipality and helped Lawrence on the farm. I ate, slept, laughed, cried, and survived.

Jodie graduated and moved on to university to become a pharmacist.

One night while working on something in the office at home, Lindsey came in, nervously sitting beside me. I wasn't ready for this talk.

"Mom . . . I think I'd like to live with Dad . . ."

My heart froze.

When she left, I was devastated. I had caused more pain, again. I would come to realize later what was happening.

I was officially at the bottom of the pit.

CHAPTER 10

I had to "get out of myself." No one attended my pity parties, so helping others seemed a good remedy. I called a nearby nursing home to meet the recreation director to ask about volunteering.

Sitting in her office, we chatted concerning ideas to help the residents. I asked what the other volunteers did.

"What other volunteers?" she said.

I read short stories to them—once a week walking throughout the nursing home, knocking on doors, pushing wheelchairs, and gathering whoever wanted to listen into a room.

One night, I noticed a bright, new, shiny, red walker outside one door as I knocked.

"I will call for someone to help me out of bed, Dear," I heard from inside.

One couple lived together in the nursing home. I said hello as they walked toward me, but their eyes did not meet mine. They didn't hear me. They were fixated on the red walker.

The walker was red, shiny, and new—the crème de la crème of walkers. If BMW or Porsche had a walker in their line of cars, this was it. It had a place to sit, a cup holder, the best brake pads, a place for "stuff," and a clear coat finish to boot.

Everything that I thought was important was flashing before me—hard work which would pay off in worldly possessions. And the harder you worked, the more "stuff" you would accumulate; you know . . . things that would increase your self-worth.

A lump formed in my throat.

The next morning, I cried telling Lawrence the story.

LIFE LESSON #13: *As life draws to a close, the things you thought were important, like money, prestige, or power, will not matter. You might have a room, a chest of drawers, and perhaps a shiny new red walker. But what will matter is how you lived your life and what you did with it.*

CHAPTER 11

I struggled within the cocoon, my spirit stirring. But the maker of the cocoon didn't notice.

A year and a half later Lindsey came back, and I felt a second chance coming my way. She came with me once in a while to the nursing home. The residents loved being read animal stories, afterward telling their own stories of pets and animals.

I asked if I could bring our basset hound to the nursing home. The staff loved the idea. Zach's debut in the common room had some residents scared to touch him; they had clearly had a bad experience with dogs. But most were ecstatic! One petted him, then the next, then the first one called him back again, and on it went. We moved on to the rooms where the residents were not mobile, hesitating before we walked into one particular room. An elderly woman lay in bed. A stroke had left her unable to speak.

I poked my head around the door. "Hi! My daughter and I are here with our dog. Would you like to see him?" I asked.

Her eyes lit up, and the biggest smile that her stroke allowed covered her face. I lifted Zach up onto the bed, her feeble arms reaching out to touch him.

A nurse walked by. "What's going on in here?" she asked.

Oh great, I thought. *Now we're in trouble.* I started to apologize.

"Stop apologizing," she said. "We have never seen her smile." Tears welled in the nurse's eyes, and the effect on Lindsey was profound. Later, she chose to work as an aide in a nursing home.

A few years went by and I experienced more health issues. When I was 35 years old, on a ski trip with my sister, Jodie surprised us by meeting us at the airport. When we landed, I was experiencing pain in my chest and couldn't breathe. After I got off the plane, Jodie looked on in horror as I collapsed.

After being rushed to the hospital by ambulance, a doctor came into the cubicle waving the ECG results, announcing a heart attack. They gave me nitroglycerin. As I laid on the gurney, bargaining with God, I asked Him what He wanted and told Him I would do whatever He asked. There was no response.

Two years later, a hysterectomy was in order. By this time, the "heart pains" had intensified enough that large doses of enteric-coated aspirin were prescribed. But I was not told soon enough before the surgery to stop taking it, and bled profusely as they rushed me back into the operating room, Lawrence and Lindsey watching in horror.

It was starting to feel as though God wasn't nudging me, He was giving me a shove.

PART III

The Awakening

CHAPTER 12

On Easter morning of 1999, Lawrence and I slept in. As usual on weekend mornings we had coffee, turning on the television to watch the news.

A reporter interviewed one of the thousands of refugees pouring out of Kosovo. Everything he had was on a horse-drawn cart. I don't recall the question the reporter asked, but I remember the refugee's answer.

"Faith will get us through this," he said.

Tears fell from my eyes, coming from a deep, stagnant well. Lawrence tenderly asked what was wrong.

"That man has nothing, and yet he has everything. I have everything, yet I have nothing."

We decided right then and there to attend church the next Sunday.

I became a sponge, needing to understand everything about this God who pursued me. I read books, had a spiritual mentor, attended study sessions, and read the Bible, its pages an extremely quenching drink for which I thirsted. In the meantime, another issue of trust had been brewing.

A friend of ours had taken a liking to Lindsey when she was about ten years of age. He started asking if he could pick her up and take her for rides in his truck. He and his wife had never had any children. It seemed perfect—he doted on her like a grandfather.

Months went by. He would come into my office and stop by the farm to visit. One night he and his wife came for supper. Within minutes, I was cringing. Something wasn't right. There he was, lying on the floor beside Lindsey, trying to engage her in conversation as she watched television. A familiar feeling swept over me. Then I noticed the look on his wife's face.

As soon as they left, Lawrence and I talked. The relationship needed to be terminated, immediately. The next time he came to my office, I gently told him that I didn't think it was a good idea for him to pick up Lindsey anymore. But week after week he kept returning, asking to see her. The asking turned to pleading. And the pleading then turned to begging.

The Rural Municipal office that I worked in was a one person office. I had never noticed before that no one else was ever in the office when he came around.

One day, after pleading with me for an extended period of time, I told him the conversation was finished and sat down at my desk. He came around the counter, got down on one knee, and began to cry and then beg some more. I had never experienced so much pressure.

Within a few days, we noticed his truck sitting by the lane into the farm. He would watch Lindsey get onto the bus, and then leave. It got so bad that as soon as I would see his truck pull up in front of my office, I would lock the door and call Lawrence. As soon as he saw Lawrence's truck, he would drive away.

Finally, I took the matter to the Royal Canadian Mounted Police. They came to the house and asked to speak with Lindsey alone. When I came back into the room, she was crying as the police officer gently urged her to tell me one of the things that had been happening.

He had been giving her money, as much as one hundred dollars at a time and telling her not to tell me. The police officer and I exchanged glances. My hunches had been correct. She was being groomed.

The officers went to "have a talk" with him.

The "visits" subsided for a time, but started again. This time, he was asked to enter a peace bond, in which he would be restrained from having any contact with Lindsey or me for a period of a year. He refused, so we would need to have a hearing.

The amount of tension, both at home and at work was unbearable. It was like a poison that seeped into every aspect of our lives.

The court date was set, January 4, 2000—Lindsey's fifteenth birthday. But a storm with freezing rain had passed through the day before. The phone rang early the day of her birthday. We were told the judge was unable to drive on the roads and the hearing was postponed.

There we were on the couch, Lawrence at one end and me at the other, with Lindsey's head cradled in my lap and Lawrence gently rubbing her feet, as we listened to her sob. There was nothing I could do but encourage her that we would get through this.

A few weeks later, we finally had our court date. After hearing all the evidence, it didn't take long for the judge to come to a decision. The peace bond was imposed.

Shortly after the year had elapsed, spring was in the air. It seemed to all finally be over, we could breathe again. Lindsey had her driver's license and was doing well. She had been seeing a psychologist who helped her wade through the emotional chaos that had reigned. But that ended the morning she came running into my office, scared and out of breath.

He had been sitting in his truck and had been watching the farm from half a mile away. As soon as Lindsey drove out of the yard, he pulled onto the grid road so that his truck would be in front of her vehicle. He stopped and would not allow her vehicle to drive by. Then he got out, walked back to her car, and started knocking on her window.

Within minutes, I drove to the RCMP office. "Either you do something, or I will," I told them. He was charged with criminal harassment, also known as stalking, and we found ourselves in court again, this time with a different prosecutor and different judge.

There was one point during the trial when I was deeply offended. His wife had not been at the trial for the peace bond, but she was at this one. One of the questions asked of her was whether or not she and her husband attended church. "Oh yes," she said.

What on earth did that have to do with anything? It was as though we all needed to conclude that if they were going to church, then he was clearly innocent. But what offended me even more was that the lawyer was bringing God into the equation. It was clear she would stop at nothing to clear her client—including playing the God card.

He was found not guilty. Words cannot describe the feelings that ensued as I once again cradled my daughter as she cried.

Thankfully we were never bothered again, and it would be years before I would be able to forgive, but I came to realize something. I should've recognized what was happening within days of him asking to pick up Lindsey for rides when she was ten, but I had not worked through any of my emotional pain of sexual abuse and didn't recognize what was happening. I had not protected my daughter. I had handed her over on a silver platter.

LIFE LESSON #14: *If you do not work through your emotional pain, you may pass it on to future generations without realizing it. Misery loves company.*

CHAPTER 13

The summer of 2000, Jodie married Aaron. On the day of the wedding, a horrendous storm brewed. Rain fell like it hadn't in a long time. As the ceremony ended, the sun broke through the clouds.

In 2004, my first grandson, Austin Jacob, arrived. Oh, how I loved him. But the birth was a stark reminder of what I had done. Never would I see the grandchildren from my aborted child. The truth hit hard. It wasn't just one child aborted, it was generations of children. A whole limb had been cut off of the family tree.

CHAPTER 14

A pamphlet arrived in the mail one day, offering a public speaking course. I enrolled.

As the course drew to a close, we were to give a five-minute speech on a project of our choosing. The calling resonated again. I spoke regarding teenagers and abstinence. Our "talks" ended with voting on whom among us, with our new public speaking abilities, would have an impact. Thirty had taken the course, and I wrote the names of the gifted individuals I thought would have the greatest impact. The winner was to be announced graduation night.

When graduation night arrived, Lawrence sat beside me as they announced my name as the winner. I was stunned. I had improved in my speaking, but I was nowhere close to the other's abilities.

That night, a woman approached me. "Ever heard of the Pregnancy Counselling Center?" she asked. "I'm sure they talk to kids about abstinence. Check it out." A few minutes later, she eerily disappeared.

I called the Pregnancy Counselling Center two weeks later. Anyone wanting to volunteer must enroll in a week-long training course. They would call when the next one took place.

Months went by until a woman called from the center. She said that my name and number was on a piece of paper, but she had no idea what it was regarding. So I told her I wanted to take the training.

"Oh good!" she exclaimed. "The Director will call to interview you. The training starts next week."

The director—a bubbly, passionate, but serious woman—called me and asked a series of questions.

"Have you ever had an abortion?"

"Yes, yes I have," I choked out.

There was no judgement, only tender compassion. She told me that a video with interviews of women who had abortions would be shown during the training. The center ran an abortion recovery program, so part of the teaching would include post-abortive grief. If I needed to leave the room, she told me she understood.

The day of the videos, my heart leaped to my mouth. Another "heart pain" attack developed. I didn't dare leave the room. Everyone present would figure out I'd had an abortion. I sat frozen to my seat, not a muscle moved until the video had ended.

During the break, I approached the director.

"I need help," I said through my tears. "I have many of the post-abortive grief symptoms."

She said she would gladly help me, but she had one more question. "Were you sexually abused as a child?"

"Yes, but it wasn't a big deal," I answered flippantly.

"Will you make an appointment with me to talk about the sexual abuse before starting the abortion recovery program?"

"Yes," I said, "but I'm telling you, it wasn't a big deal."

Days later, I sat trying to convince her once again.

"Where would you place yourself on a scale of one to ten—ten being the best regarding how much you love yourself?" she asked.

An eternity went by. Closing my eyes, I desperately tried to hold back the tears.

"I can't even put myself on the scale . . . I'm such a basket case!"

"No, you are a woman who has a few baskets. And I will help you get through each one," she whispered.

She asked me to journal, so I took her advice and journaled my thoughts throughout the healing process. Here are some excerpts from those first few months:

March 3, 2004 – Being molested as a child is a big deal. I must accept that. I've been dancing around it for a long time. Help me, God, to work through this instead of continually around it. After talking with Karen yesterday, I see how I've been in denial. If it happened to one of my children, I would be mortified. What a revelation! I have been misleading myself!

March 4, 2004 – I've been thinking of what Karen said about me protecting Lindsey, Jodie, and Austin, but who would protect me? I must admit, the first thought was that I didn't deserve protection, as though I'm the one to blame for what happened. I'm trying to look from the outside in. It's a stupid statement to blame a child. One thing is for sure, I'm damaged goods. I can't see myself ever telling Lawrence. He would never want to touch me again. A lot of times that would be fine because I don't like to be touched! But I do want to be loved by him.

March 5, 2004 – I looked up information on childhood sexual abuse. Checking off from the list of after-effects, I'm understanding how "big of a deal" this really is. I have been promiscuous. I have trouble saying no, but an inability to trust people. No wonder I don't trust that God has forgiven me! I always feel guilt, shame, fear, and anxiety and am a "control at all costs" person. I have problems giving or receiving affection and find it difficult to rely on others, always trying to be perfect. I have physical symptoms with no medical cause and a high pain tolerance. I have problems with alcohol. I put up with criticism from others. I prefer to stay at home. I tend to sexualize thoughts and at times humor is sexual. I have a problem with compulsive spending. I have had an unplanned pregnancy. So yes, this has affected my life, and has opened my eyes and made me realize the reasons for many of my actions when I was young. Lawrence and I laid awake in the middle of the night. He told me how much he loved me. He told me how proud he was of me and that he knew God was doing great things in my life and had great things in store. He said he hoped he would be around long enough to share in the glory for God. I've been reading excerpts of the "Purpose Driven Life" to him. He told me he appreciated it and how inspiring it was. He said he was very proud to have me as his wife. If only he could have seen the tears sliding down my cheeks. Thank God it was dark. I was dying inside. I'm trying hard to be that person but it was not me he was talking about.

March 9, 2004 – God, I don't understand why you would allow something like this to happen. Other issues have been my choice but this happening when I was a child was not a choice of mine. If you care so much for the children, how could You allow me to hurt like that? I don't understand. A book I'm reading says we endure pain or You allow pain as a wake-up call. Was this supposed to be a wake-up call? Why would You allow something that would have me having all kinds of trust problems? Why should I trust You when you didn't take care of me then? If this is the beginning of a closer relationship with You God, I guess we've started. If one way of being closer to You is to be honest and frank, I just poured out a lot of honesty and frankness.

March 10, 2004 – Reading more on sexual abuse healing, it talked of going through the grief process and the sadness associated with it. While reading, a profound sense of sadness came over me for the childhood I didn't have. Was the reason for the pregnancy at fifteen that I subconsciously knew if I had a child, my childhood would be over? If I couldn't stand what was happening, wouldn't I want it to be over as soon as possible? The article said the healing process can take a long time. God, I ask that You help me to be patient with myself and to trust You know the best path to take for this healing to take place. I pray I'll be a freer, better person who will enjoy what You have blessed me with so I can let others know what a loving God You are.

March 11, 2004 – The book says we are to worship God, even when we do not feel His presence and that God is always there. Again I feel betrayed. If You were watching every detail why didn't You stop it? Am I being selfish for these thoughts? I've always been an advocate of "everything happens for a reason." Why can't I accept that this was allowed to happen? Why do I want to protect my abuser? I do not understand! Why would I want to protect him when no one was around to protect me? I'm having a hard time with this.

March 12, 2004 – When thinking about this, (which is only when I'm writing in this journal), a rage builds inside, deep in the pit of my stomach. It's not strong, but it's there.

April 2, 2004 – A week ago, I told Lawrence. That was something I never thought I would do. Even though it was hard, a heavy burden has lifted. The truth does *set you free. We've had a rocky road but I am certain Lawrence loves me for who I am and if not, God is there and loves me unconditionally, even with everything I've done. I've been learning about how God allows experiences to enable us to comfort others. I read and reread a few paragraphs of that chapter ten times. We are to use painful experiences to serve others, especially the ones we want to hide and forget. It helps to know that. Even though I haven't wanted to share this experience or my abortion experience with any-one, I understand why God allowed them. 2 Corinthians 1:3–4 opened my eyes. There are other people that couldn't handle what I've gone through and I couldn't handle what others have gone through. Even though I don't understand all of Your ways God, I am accepting that everything happens for a reason. Even though I'm not ready to comfort those with these experiences, I know You have been preparing me. I hope and pray as I learn to love and serve You in the ways You intended, Lawrence will be there for me and grow with me. I am slowly accepting who I am and because I know Your love is inexhaustible. God, I can now place myself as a two on the scale of self-worth. Coming to terms with telling others about my life will be a challenge, but if that's what Your will is for me God, I will do it.*

May 4, 2004 – Karen asked how I felt when thinking of being a young child in that situation. From the "emotions sheet," I picked overwhelmed, frustrated, and fearful. She asked if I felt violated. I responded yes. So here I am journaling about being violated. The dictionary says: To break intentionally or unintentionally; disregard—to injure the person or property of; to rape; to do harm to property or qualities considered sacred; desecrate—too disturb rudely or improperly; interrupt.

Yes, violated is the word. My spirit broke. A child, I was inno-cent, as white as snow. That was taken. He took what was mine when I was not ready to give it—my sexuality. What greater gift can a woman give a man? I could no longer give that gift. Even now, coldness emanates from me. But it didn't matter that he took something from me. He cared only of himself, his desires, his wants, his needs. I am a human being! I have a soul! I was created by God! But that did not matter. I am not a plaything for someone else's pleasure! I had no control over what happened. I keep having this vision of this caped figure descending, an evil force I cannot fight. Or a vision of a big hawk, spreading its wings and descending on a little creature. The creature has no clue what will happen. I sat there unknowing and so trusting. The trust broke.

Yes, violated is the word. Oh how I've been injured, raped of my dignity as a person. You cannot see the injuries, but they run deep. It scarred for life, affecting me in so many ways. Now I'm picking away at the scar tissue and revealing the injuries. I went through life minimizing it so I wouldn't have to deal with the pain of the injury. Injuries showed up in how I conducted myself; by being promiscuous, as though of no value, as though feelings didn't matter. Injuries showed up in being unable to communicate with young children. Injuries showed up in being unable to accept an honest hug from someone other than my husband or even a pat on the shoulder or a touch of the hand without jumping out of my skin. Injuries showed up in being unable to accept God's forgiveness for my sins because I felt I had no value. I was not worth being forgiven. Injuries showed up in being unable to have a normal sex life with my husband. Injuries showed up in almost not protecting my own child from sexual abuse. Injuries showed up by telling myself the human being with a soul growing inside of me was just a blob of tissue with no value either. Injuries showed up by being so depressed, I wished myself dead. No, you cannot see my injuries, but my heart and soul broke and I am just now mending.

Yes, violated is the word. A woman's sexuality is sacred. It is not something to be given away frivolously. It is what makes a woman pure. It is something to be prized and valued. Mine was desecrated and stolen. A woman's sexuality is something so pure and sacred; God says it should only be touched by a man whom God has chosen as a gift to the woman. Their relationship sanctified in a ceremony so precious, God says the only relationship greater is one with Him.

Finally, yes, violated is the word. My life as a child was interrupted. Everything seemed to mushroom from there. I cannot say this event is to blame for the problems in my life, but it is a reference point to things sliding from that point on. I am not a "thing" to be used and thrown away. My body is not an inanimate object as though separate from my mind and soul. Body, mind, and soul are interconnected. When one part is injured, the other parts are affected. My soul hurt; otherwise, I would not have turned from God so many times or thought so little of myself. My mind could not deal with it until now.

May 6, 2004 – I can see now I had just tucked everything away in the closet. Now I'm resentful toward Mom. There is no doubt I was crying out for help when playing with the matches. I needed my parents to protect me, but they weren't there. Deep down, did Mom know something was wrong and couldn't handle it, so she kept hitting me until she heard what she wanted to hear? I betrayed my friend. My mother made me betray my friend. Why would you do that Mom? You were supposed to be a mom and figure out why I would do something like that. I had always envisioned my childhood as being somewhat idyllic but I guess it's the way I wanted to remember so it wouldn't hurt. I think Mom went through a lot in her own childhood that she's not dealing with. But pretending everything is okay doesn't make it go away. Did I act out as a teenager to get back at you Mom? I hope parents can deal with their own crap so they don't pass it down from generation to generation. I will do my part to make sure it doesn't happen from this point. Facing myself has not been easy, and it will not get easier soon. But I'm tired of walking around the pain. I want to walk through it to a brighter future.

LIFE LESSON #15: When we look through the trash of our lives, we will find ugly puzzle pieces that made us who we are. They're smelly and ugly, but until we find them, we will never understand ourselves. And understanding is a huge part of healing.

May 10, 2004 – Well, yesterday was Mother's Day. I reflected on the mother I was to Jodie and Lindsey and realized I lacked in so many respects. I don't know why Mom and I could never talk. It was never a part of our relationship. I've concluded that if I need forgiveness from my children for not being a good mom, then I need to forgive my own mom. As the eldest child, I'm sure she didn't want to let down her parents. She always had to do the "right" thing and appear good in people's eyes. I talked with Mom when she came out to visit. Karen was right again. I needed to get to know her better. I do honor you, Mom, and I do love you.

May 24, 2004 – Lawrence and I talked at length. I told him how my emotions are an entangled necklace and I'm now picking it apart. He feels so bad for everything I went through as a child, but I told him I'm not interested in a pity party. I am grateful I could tell him this and yet angry I should have to go through it in the first place. Karen asked me to journal about picking up stones. I judge people and throw stones so they can't know me. I won't allow them to come close; otherwise they will be repulsed, like Lawrence was at first. Now he is becoming very supportive. I'm seeing a need to be in control of men. If I run into one who is uncontrollable, it makes me upset. What's funny is it's probably the same from their point of view! I have to do something physical to release these emotions, such as walking or something. I've started on this journey and can't go back now. For the first time, I'm feeling real. It's because I'm not pretending anymore and that's okay. There is no need to put on a facade at home anymore. I can fall apart if I want to.

May 28, 2004 – I'm not looking forward to talking to my abuser. I'm not sure why I'm afraid. Why am I so afraid of speaking the truth? Wouldn't it be better to finally be real? Funny thing, I've been gaining weight. Is it my way of protecting myself? I do not want to deal with this. I have felt so ashamed. A book I'm reading explains, "Shame exists in an environment of secrecy." I do not want to be ashamed anymore. God, I do not want to be ashamed anymore! I have lived with the fear of people finding out what happened and the things I've done. I would rather someone respect and like me for who I am, not for who they think I am.

LIFE LESSON #16: The truth sets you free.

Sunday, May 30, 2004 – Today is Pentecost Sunday. In church, they talked of our need to know God has forgiven us and of our need to forgive others. God spoke to my heart, telling me I needed to forgive. God has forgiven me so much. If He forgave everything I've done, how could I not forgive? If there was ever anyone who needed forgiveness, it's me. Is it not possible my abuser could think the same way? I'm right in the middle of the pain now. I can see how far I've come and can see to the other side. What matters now is where I go from here. If God has forgiven me for what I've done, and if I can forgive those who trespassed against me, then I can start out with a new slate, can't I? How exciting is that?

I wrote a letter to the person who had abused me, telling him I forgave him. I carried it around in my purse for three days until I found the courage to put it in the mailbox.

Within a few days, the phone rang. He wanted to meet to talk about the letter.

June 4, 2004 – I talked to him on the phone. I felt empowered. I don't know what to say when we talk but God will watch out for me. Whatever happens now happens. I'm responsible for my actions and he is responsible for his. I'm being catapulted into the present and I'm leaving the past behind. We grow spiritually, the same as how we get into shape physically. It takes a lot of work. "No pain, no gain." There will be an incredible amount of gain through the pain I'm suffering now.

We met. I forgave him in person. The taste of freedom was palpable, and I wanted more of it.

LIFE LESSON #17: *Mark 11:26 says, "But if you do not forgive, neither will your Father in heaven forgive your transgressions" (NKJV). Ouch. I need to pray for those who have hurt me, but if they remain unrepentant, they will inevitably have to answer not to me . . . but to God, the Maker of the Universe.*

Whenever I think of this life lesson a picture forms in my mind; I'm holding a large number of helium balloons which will lift me closer to God. But in my other hand, I have a hook. And that hook is in the people that I have not yet forgiven for hurting me or my family. As long as my "bitterness" hook remains, I will not allow myself to draw closer to God. So, in reality, this is not about my relationship with the person who has trespassed against me. It is about my relationship with God.

CHAPTER 15

It was time to move on to the next basket. Through the post-abortive program at the center, I met with another woman who experienced an abortion. Karen, the center's director who guided me through the sexual abuse pain, facilitated our meetings.

As we moved through denial, anger, guilt, shame, forgiveness, and acceptance, I could sense God holding my hand, guiding me through the darkness.

LIFE LESSON #18: *There is a huge difference between guilt and shame. God uses guilt to turn us to repentance. If we have sinned, He wants us to feel remorse for what we have done. Shame is what Satan uses to make you feel bad about yourself as a person so you will never turn to God. God loves you but hates your sin. Satan loves your sin and hates God.*

July 4, 2004 – What a great session with Karen yesterday. God was present. Karen talked about Paul and David, and the sins God forgave them for. But I had problems accepting God's forgiveness when thinking of them. They were men. I'm a woman. Women are supposed to give life, not take it. She reminded me men are supposed to protect it. That statement hit like a brick. I took all the responsibility and rested it on my shoulders. I realized why I had been picking up so many stones and throwing them at men. She also reminded me that nowhere in the Bible does it say God forgives all sin except abortion. He does not place a caveat on His word. I have been allowing Satan to tell my heart God could not forgive me—that I should stay shameful. I have been walking in darkness. How can others recognize

forgiveness if those of us who have been forgiven say nothing? I'm
beginning to understand how Satan works. I'm understanding
the difference between shame and regret. My actions regarding
the abortion were shameful, but I should not continue to bear
shame if I have repented and received God's forgiveness. It would
be shameful of me to think I had done nothing wrong. What I
should be sensing is regret. I know God wants me to speak out
about this. He wants to show others they can be forgiven and can
experience the full forgiveness and love of God. Someone needs to
tell women the line society has been feeding them is a lie. This is
not a "blob of tissue." This is a human being with a God-created
soul. It will take a while to rid myself of the shameful feelings. I
perceive in my head God has forgiven. I'm just now recognizing
it in my heart. It hit hard when Karen said that God is crying
because I will not recognize His forgiveness. If He sent Jesus to
endure everything before and during His crucifixion so I could
be forgiven, it's like I'm saying He went through it all for nothing.
Or that it wasn't enough and He should do it again. I can't help
feeling an incredible amount of love with that statement. Jesus
went through that so I can be forgiven. When leaving the center
last night, I wanted to shout from the rooftops! I wanted to hug
everyone in sight! I want to let everyone know they need not go
through life in pain.

July 5, 2004 – 1 John 2:1–2 "My dear children, I write this to you
so that you will not sin. But if anyone does sin, we have one who
speaks to the Father in our defense—Jesus Christ, the righteous
one. He is the atoning sacrifice for our sins and not only for ours,
but also for the sins of the whole world." Oh Jesus, I want you
to be able to stand in my defense. Help me to experience your
forgiveness. Oh God, I want to be as white as snow. God, help me
make Your joy complete. After reading the Bible I was reminded
of excerpts from Psalm 51: "Have mercy on me, O God, accord-
ing to your unfailing love; according to your great compassion

blot out my transgressions. Wash away all my iniquity and cleanse me from my sin. For I know my transgressions and my sin is always before me. . . . Cleanse me with hyssop and I will be clean, wash me and I will be whiter than snow. . . . Then I will teach transgressors your ways and sinners will turn back to you" (vs. 1–3, 7, 13).

As we prepared for a memorial for our aborted children, Thanksgiving was approaching. Jodie and Aaron invited us for Thanksgiving supper.

The memorial for my aborted child was extremely important. I named him Jedidiah. It was time to honor him. It was time to show respect for the soul that God had created. I wanted my children to be there. That meant I must tell them I aborted their sibling.

I was anxious the whole evening of Thanksgiving. After supper, I asked them if I could talk to them. In my heart, I was taking a huge risk. What if they never spoke to me again? But I sensed strongly what God was asking me to do.

I told them what happened, and it was as though I repented all over again, waves of grief shaking my body. Jodie and Lindsey got up from their chairs. Were they leaving the room? Were they walking out of my life forever? They sat, one on either side of me, and held me as we cried together. They told me how much they loved me. They told me they forgave me.

And they said something unforgettable. They always sensed something or someone was missing. I realized again how much I had altered our family. Jodie should have two siblings. Lindsey should be the middle child, not the youngest.

CHAPTER 16

The day of the memorial arrived. I played a particular song that had come to mean so much to me—"Love Song" by Third Day. "Just to be with you, there's no price I didn't pay. Just to be with you, I gave My Life away." Then I read the poem I wrote:

Prayer for Jedidiah

When I was very young, I had this dream,
I was walking on a path in some sand far away,
I hadn't thought of it much until this day.

This being walked beside me on this path,
I knew that He cared very deeply for me,
Beside me always He wanted to be.

The being only loved me, He did not judge,
While I was with Him, my heart leapt and soared,
I knew that this being was Jesus Christ, our Lord.

I went on with my life and I searched everywhere,
I wanted to feel what I felt with Him,
I stumbled and fell, my light started to dim.

With child I was, bad timing I thought,
Never again would I be on that path in that place,
I made the wrong choice, and I fell from grace.

Oh God, please help me take back what I've done!
I woke up screaming in anguish and pain,
My life would never be the same again.

I would give anything if You just put him back!
Awaken me from this nightmare, I cried!
But nothing stirred in my womb, all life had died.

What I had done! This was God's child, not mine!
I was told by so many it was my choice to make,
But this innocent soul was not mine to take.

For years this sin has hung on my neck,
Deep shame and guilt have taken their toll,
It's weighed very heavy on my heart, mind and soul.

Forgiveness is something I do not deserve,
Many people would say that my soul is lost,
You did it yourself, now you must pay the cost!

Lord, I am not worthy to whisper your name,
My shadow is long and my sins are great,
I said long ago I accepted my fate.

For years God patiently waited for me,
He said I loved you then and I still love you now,
I'll give you the strength to get through this somehow.

God said I forgave you the first time you asked,
No sin is too great for Me to forget,
My son paid the ultimate price for your debt.

I am the sinful woman, the woman at the well,
A prodigal daughter who feels His embrace,
Am I back in the sand, on that path, in that place?

Jesus, they're my tears that wash your feet,
I carefully dry them with my hair,
God said He sent you for my solace and care.

God told me I'm free! He had wiped my slate clean!
He told me He heard all the prayers that I said,
For all of my sins, that's why His son bled.

It can all be said in a song that I know,
To be with me there's no price He didn't pay,
To be with me, He gave His life away.

God said please meet the creation I made,
He's in heaven with Me and he's doing just fine,
Jedidiah's his name, beloved one of Mine.

I want to teach others that God's word is truth,
Lord, use me as your vessel to save someone from pain,
Jed, I will not let your death be in vain.

I remember the dream that I had long ago,
God walking with me on a path in the sand,
The only difference now is I've taken His hand.

I'll worship you God all the days of my life,
Such peace and joy my heart has never known,
Heaven's waiting for me, and Jed will never be alone.

For so long, my heart was heavy with Condemnation, Punishment, and Rejection. But God did CPR. He revived my heart. He restored my soul. Now Compassion, Protection, and Restoration reigned. CPR.

Lawrence did not attend the memorial. He perceived it something my children and I should do alone. That night, we talked of the day's events. I was physically and emotionally exhausted. I headed for bed, blowing out the candles before leaving the room. Lawrence stayed up for a while before coming to bed.

At 3:00 a.m., I awoke to a glow. I tiptoed into the living room, unsure of what I would find. One candle still burned, emitting the most beautiful glow. A peace I had never known surrounded me. I sat in His presence. He was close. Two years later, I phoned the hospital to ask for the actual date of the abortion. The day I had picked for the memorial was the anniversary date of the abortion. Only God could have set that up.

My spirit continued to struggle. It began to emerge from the darkness of its cocoon.

CHAPTER 17

Karen trained six to be post-abortive facilitators. One day, we talked of what could be done to reach post-abortive women.

I slammed my fist on the table. "Someone needs to start talking about this!" I shouted.

"Well maybe that someone needs to be you," Karen retorted.

"Oh no, I can't ever see myself doing that," I said, shaking my head. But something stirred. He was calling, asking me to struggle further out of the cocoon. I told Lawrence I believed God was calling me to share my story. To my surprise, he felt the same.

Karen resigned at the Pregnancy Counselling Center and her assistant, Lorraine, was hired as the new director, and a date was set for me to share at a church for the first time.

My knees knocked, emotion pouring out of me. There wasn't a dry eye in the place. The next day, as I relived the night, Satan tried desperately to renew the shame. It was as though I had stood naked before them, with nothing to cover myself.

With much encouragement from Lorraine, I shared at a few more churches and also became the facilitator of the post-abortive program at the center on a volunteer basis.

I also called churches in the area where I lived as well as the city, introducing myself as the post-abortive facilitator for the Options Pregnancy Center, asking to share with the congregation as a healed post-abortive woman. I reiterated the importance for other post-abortive women to see someone standing before them, healed.

The minister of one church said she was pro-choice, and that nowhere in the Bible did it say that abortion wasn't okay. If I stood in front of her congregation talking about the post-abortive program, she thought the women present might get the impression that an abortion they had was wrong. She said abortion did not require forgiveness. My jaw dropped.

I was gracious as I bowed out of the conversation on the phone, but the day marked the end of my "religious naivety." The minister I spoke with was of the same denomination whose elders told Dad not to bother to bring his children to Sunday school unless he paid his tithes.

I dropped to my knees and thanked God the denomination had not corrupted my thoughts as a child. And I prayed for the post-abortive women in that church. What would they do with their guilt?

LIFE LESSON #19: *If you experience guilt, listen to your gut instinct. It is highly likely the Holy Spirit leading you. Do not trust people. Trust God.*

CHAPTER 18

January 10, 2006, my second grandson, Alex Wesley, was born. Jodie and Aaron chose his second name after Dad. It was the greatest honor they could give. I smiled from ear to ear.

Later that month, Lorraine called me at work. "A woman wants to take a team of post-abortive women to set up a workshop at the United Nations in New York. You should go, Melony. When she called, I thought of you right away."

I wondered if she had fallen off her rocker! I would have to go more public with my story. People in the small town of 300 residents close to where we lived, would find out. But the more I pondered, the more I sensed something pushing me to go.

"Oh God," I prayed, "Are you serious? How will people react?"

As I started to embrace the call to speak at the UN workshop in New York, an idea formed—a plan for a silent auction of jewelry I would make as a fundraiser for New York. Hopefully, many women would come. I attended a Bible study with some local women, all different denominations, yet so clearly sisters in Christ. I would have to enlist their help. But there was an addition to the night few were aware of—the sharing of my testimony.

I called my friend Judy, the leader of the Bible study, to share the idea. She was excited to hear of the trip. It was time for the hard part, why was I going? Because I had first-hand experience with the topic we would be sharing in New York. The silence was deafening. She shared later that her jaw dropped to the floor. Her voice trembled, but there was absolutely no judgement. She wanted to help.

The night of the auction came on February 22, 2006. The local town hall filled. Jodie and Lindsey came to support me as well as Karen and Lorraine from the center. The Bible study group organized everything. I stood in the kitchen of the hall, my whole body shaking.

At the microphone, I looked at Jodie, Lindsey, and the women there, knowing everything was going to change at that moment. I started to speak, and told my whole story. Tears filled the room from every corner.

That night, Karen stayed overnight with me. We sat by the fire. It was late, but the phone rang. It was one of the local women who had attended the auction. She was very agitated.

"My daughter was sitting at the kitchen table when I got home tonight," she said, "I told her about everything you shared. Then she dropped a bombshell. She told me a friend is having an abortion in the morning and she is going with her to support her."

She continued on, talking so fast I had to ask her to slow down a couple of times. "My daughter is going to drive to her friend's place. She wants to know if it's okay to call later if her friend will talk to you?"

I said Karen could talk with her if they called. At two o'clock in the morning, the phone rang. The friend was willing to talk. At once, I handed it to Karen.

Karen spoke gently, asking the young woman how she was feeling and what her circumstances were. I sat there, listening to Karen's side of the conversation, my spirit holding its breath.

Karen listened, responding with a calm, soothing voice. "My friend Melony shared her testimony in her home town tonight. I think you should talk to her." She handed me the phone.

"No!" I whispered as I shook my head back and forth. "I can't do that!"

I took the phone, covering the mouthpiece. "Are you crazy?" I whispered vehemently again, eyes wide. "I can talk to a post-abortive woman, but I cannot talk to this woman!"

"Melony, just tell her your story. You'll be fine," Karen said.

I gestured again. I could not do it! But she continued to sit there, calmly waiting. Taking the phone, I prayed the girl couldn't hear the nervousness in my voice. "I understand you're scheduled for an abortion tomorrow morning," I stammered. "Can I tell you about my experience?"

The more I shared, the more our hearts connected. She sniffled quietly as I spoke.

"God cares very deeply about what's happening here," I said. "What are the chances of us sitting here talking at 2:00 a.m. the day before you're scheduled for an abortion?"

"I thought of that," the young woman said, "and I prayed to God tonight to give me a sign."

"I think we can safely say God has done that," I whispered.

She started to sob. "I don't think I can do it," she said. "I don't think I can have this abortion."

I sat in awe of God when the conversation ended. The next morning, she canceled the appointment to abort her child.

LIFE LESSON #20: *The disciples did not recognize Jesus after He had risen until He made a simple gesture. He revealed His nail-pierced hands and the scar in His side. And this is how people recognize Him today, when men and women who have experienced the healing of past wounds are not ashamed to show their scars to a hurting world.** *

CHAPTER 19

In March of 2006, Denise Mountenay, myself, and another woman conducted the first-ever workshop on post-abortive pain at the United Nations in New York City.

For three days we trekked the hallways of the UN, inviting people. Many times, I would minister to a woman after inviting her to the workshop. I quickly learned that post-abortive emotional and spiritual pain is no respecter of race, color, creed, religion, or economic status. If a woman or a man has experienced abortion, there is pain.

LIFE LESSON #21: *Emotional and spiritual pain is no respecter of race, color, creed, religion, or economic status.*

---

*Sharon Jayne, *Your Scars Are Beautiful to God: Finding Peace and Purpose in the Hurts of Your Past* (Eugene, OR: Harvest House Publishers, 2006)

While we were in New York, we took half a day to sight-see. We went to Ground Zero, the spot where the World Trade Center once stood. As I stood there, I thought of the pain the families who lost loved ones continued to face. And the pain of the millions of families who lost loved ones they would never meet due to abortion. Those who died at Ground Zero and children who were aborted shared something in common. Both died as a result of someone else's actions.

The rest of the year, something tugged at me. And in the spring of 2007, I relented and gave in to the God who pursued me my whole life and His Son who kept saying, "Come and work for me."

I had closed the office door at the Rural Municipality for the last time. The chains had broken. I was now free and had emerged from the cocoon that had bound me for so long. Now was the time to learn how to fly.

PART IV

The Calling

CHAPTER 20

I helped Lawrence on the farm and puttered around the house doing things I previously never took time to do when I was working full-time. I also continued volunteering as the post-abortive group facilitator at the center.

Lorraine resigned as director and a woman who worked there took over the position. But she never believed she should be the director. She approached me one day, saying she was resigning. The Board of Options wondered if I was interested, I told them I was not.

Karen and I had become good friends. A few months later, the subject of the center came up. The position of director still vacant. "Are you going to apply?" she asked.

"No," I replied. "I'm not interested."

The conversation turned to other things, but she soon brought it up again. "Melony, I really think you should apply for the position."

"Karen, I am not interested! It's an hour drive from here!"

Just before the conversation ended, she brought it up again.

"For the last time Karen, I'm telling you I am not applying."

I mentioned the conversation to Lawrence. Winter was fast approaching, and we both looked forward to being home together. In the spring, I would search for a part-time job.

The next morning, a Sunday, I woke up with a start, recounting the conversation with Karen. She asked three times if I would apply. Three times I said no. I realized someone else denied Christ three times before the cock crowed. God spiritually punched me in the eyes.

I emailed the Board Chairman the same morning, tentatively applying for the position. I told him that if I were hired, changes would be made. I gave every reason not to hire me.

After church, I checked the email. The response said, "We are thrilled to have you as director!" That day, roosters became a decorating theme in my home.

November 16, 2007 was my first day at the center as director. I had closed the office door at the Rural Municipality exactly seven months to the day, earlier.

CHAPTER 21

Alone in the center the first day, the phone rang. I looked at it with dread. It was the counselling line. "Oh God, I am not prepared for this! Please help me! You've made a dreadful mistake God! Let me go back to my volunteer position as post-abortive group facilitator! I was comfortable doing that! I will screw this up! I can't do this!"

But I did it. And the more often the phone rang, the more comfortable I became. Leigh-Anne, a co-worker at the center, spoke with the abortion-minded women during counselling appointments.

One day, a woman made an appointment for the afternoon. She wanted to bring her partner. They came up the stairs with two children. Leigh-Anne needed to speak to the parents alone, so I asked if I could take the children to another room.

The office was undergoing the changes that I said I would bring. Only one room sufficed for the children—the back room. Everything had been pushed into the center of the room, to prepare for a fresh coat of paint. So on that cold November day, I sat there in the disheveled room, reading a book to the two children, while their parents spoke with Leigh-Anne about aborting their sibling.

How can this be happening? I thought. My mind flew through all the "what if's" that came from what would've happened if Dale and I had gone to a Pregnancy Counselling Center on that cold November day twenty-two years earlier.

But this time it ended differently. The couple decided to keep their baby.

CHAPTER 22

Within a month, Leigh-Anne resigned. She had pondered leaving for months, and now it was a reality. Being the only one left at the center, I was forced to see clients.

I listened to young women quietly weeping on the phone, not knowing where to turn. I saw the guilt and shame of a woman who had experienced abortion. I saw the guilt and shame of a man who had experienced abortion. I listened to the sobs of a grandmother who found out her grandchild had been aborted. I was berated on the phone by a client's aunt after finding out her niece decided to have her child. "I obviously sent my niece to the wrong place," she had said with disgust.

In January, three months after starting as director at the center, I spent a week away taking training for new directors. I returned with things to be done and ideas to implement. The direction was clear.

Each time the phone rang, we gave out hope. I sensed it in a young woman when telling her I understood because I had been there. I saw a spark of hope in a woman when I revealed I was adopted. I saw it in a post-abortive woman's eyes when telling her love and forgiveness were waiting for her if she opened the door. God was imprinting His fingerprints throughout the center.

And I knew that the aunt who called saying she sent her niece to the wrong place had sent her to the right one.

I knew that pain was no respecter of race, color, creed, religion, or economic status, and this seed of wisdom planted in me so long ago continued to grow. Women came who were black, white, yellow, red, Protestant, Catholic, Muslim, Hindu—women who were homeless and rode the rails across the country, professors, housewives, police, teachers, nurses, students, women who wanted to abort after they gave birth to an earlier in vitro child only to become pregnant naturally months later, couples who invited others into their bedroom, women who weren't sure who the father was, women who had aborted their father's child, and so many more.

Many times, I shared my testimony in churches. In Catholic churches, inevitably a woman would come up to me afterward and say, "Can you please pray for my sister? She's an evangelical."

In evangelical churches, a woman would say, "Can you please pray for my sister? She's a Catholic."

LIFE LESSON #22: The evil one loves to use the wedge of denominations to separate. If Jesus Christ is your Savior, then you are my sister or brother in Christ. I highly doubt there will be different gates to enter Heaven.

One hot, summer, Friday afternoon in 2008, I took time off in the afternoon. I had been working hard at the center and went home to mow the lawn. Lawrence had just fixed the lawn mower, and it was working great. Client calls after hours were forwarded to the cell phone 24/7 and it was in my pocket. The mower broke again and as I swore at it, I checked the phone, horrified to see the light blinking. A missed call! Thankfully the young woman left a message a few minutes earlier.

She had called the center two weeks earlier, but could not come in. Instead, I spent forty-five minutes on the phone with her. She had already had one abortion, her boyfriend left her, she was without a home, and without a job. She had one child already, and she could not handle another baby. She was calling to let me know she had decided to abort. I asked if she could come to the center. She could not.

I sensed God nudging me. "I can come to your place and we can talk."

"There's no need to do that," she said. "I've made my decision."

"I understand, but I want to remind you we're here for you no matter what you decide. I want to see you because I care and because you're worth it."

To my surprise, she said, "Yes."

I got cleaned up and jumped into the car. She lived two hours away. Lawrence said, "Why are you doing this? She'll probably have an abortion anyway."

I thought so too, but I had to be obedient to what God was asking me to do. He either wanted to teach her something, or me.

She called again while I was driving. "I don't think you should come. You're wasting your time."

"I'm already on the way," I told her. A few seconds went by, which seemed like an eternity, and she quietly said, "Okay."

We talked for an hour. She needed to know someone cared. She needed to be shown that she was worth it, no matter what the outcome. Two weeks later I called, and her father answered the phone. "Are you the lady that was here two weeks ago?" he asked.

I quietly answered, "Yes . . . yes I am."

"Well then, you should know she decided to have the baby."

There are no words to describe the sensation that coursed through me at those words. I spoke to her a week later, and she sounded different. She had found a job and a place to live. She had hope. She had hope for her unborn child. And hope for herself.

I thanked God that the lawnmower broke that day.

Women continued to come into the center, sometimes with their boyfriends or husbands joining them. I began to see a common thread. If the woman had low self-worth, she attracted someone of the same "worth." I started asking where they placed themselves on the "worth" scale from one to ten, ten being the best—the same question Karen had asked. Typically, they didn't place themselves high and if they did, it was clear they didn't believe it.

LIFE LESSON #23: *Water seeks its own level. If you think little of yourself or don't think you are "worth" much because of what you have been through, you will attract someone who doesn't think much of you either.*

One day, a woman brought her daughter into the center for a pregnancy test. She was twelve years old. I silently gasped when I found out her age, but had learned not to show any emotion when people said things. The girl sat chewing her bubble gum, oblivious to what was happening in her womb.

After we talked, the woman said she could not force her daughter to abort. She would do everything possible to support her. I shuddered when thinking that her daughter could have aborted without her mother's consent. But abortion is not an eraser. The answer is abstinence.

Many people coming into the center used various methods of birth control and were still getting pregnant, including those using the pill. And the numbers of women coming into the center wanting a pregnancy test—already pregnant—who had used no birth control were staggering.

One of the standard questions to ask was, "If you weren't using any birth control, did you subconsciously want to be pregnant?" The response was the same. They looked as though they were asked if they wanted to jump off a cliff.

Something much deeper was happening. And birth control was not the answer. This young girl blowing bubbles had searched for in a man what she had lacked. She thought a man could give her joy and self-worth, but it couldn't be found. Only God can give that.

CHAPTER 23

I had started teaching those coming into the center about anger. There is a part of the brain called the limbic system, which holds all of our memories. It has no concept of time. The frontal cortex of the brain is where all decisions are made, but is not fully developed until our early twenties. But the limbic system is fully formed at birth. Even though our decisions are made in the frontal cortex of the brain, the decisions are "filtered" through the limbic system. When we are presented with something that has traumatized us in the past, this can trigger a fight, flight, or freeze reaction. Most of the time, a person doesn't even realize what's happening. The traumatic event may have happened as a child or even an infant, but it is imbedded in the memory of the limbic system.

We talked about how a "trigger" from an experience could be a sound, smell, sight—anything that lights a spark and arouses an emotion. The body releases chemicals to prepare for fight, flight, or freeze mode. And unless we are aware of what's happening, we will *react* instead of *respond*. The usual reaction is not a pretty one and anger can explode in all directions. If we can find a way to use up the surge of energy coming in, then we can take time later to figure out what the trigger was. Once the trigger is found, it begins to lose its power.

One night, as I prepared supper, Lawrence entered the kitchen. We chatted about the day's events and other menial things.

"Hunting season starts tomorrow," he said. Within thirty minutes of this comment, we were in a full-fledged argument over nothing. I screamed at him as I slammed the bedroom door. Hours went by as I sobbed into my pillow.

After I recovered, I realized it was time to start practicing what I was preaching. I prayed and asked God to show me what the trigger was that caused my anger. It wasn't until the next day that my eyes grew wide with a memory that surfaced of that hunter at the corner of the road when I was ten. Even though the man had not physically touched me, he had tried his hardest to lure me into his car, and the fear of that event had remained hidden in my body for years. The darkness had been exposed. This was what had set me off. I started using the story as the perfect example of a trigger.

LIFE LESSON #24: If a person has sustained trauma in their life, the body and soul remember the incident and there will be triggers.

CHAPTER 24

I continued to connect the dots with clients, realizing over and over again that if people kept adding pain into their "emotional cup," it would spill over and *affect* not just themselves, but it would *infect* everyone around them.

In one portion of the post-abortive program, women drew or described in words what their "emotional wound" looked like. It helped to gaze at it again at the end to show how far they had come in their healing. One woman described her wound in these words: "It is a cold, depressing darkness that wants to suck me in. There is ugliness all around me, and I can smell vomit and blood." What kind of impact would she have on those around her if this was going on inside?

After finishing the program, she described her wound as, "I am sealed with forgiveness; I am loved; I feel complete; I feel light and hopeful; I have a future of glory." She had a far different impact on her family and others from that point forward.

Emotional pain from abortion has far reaching effects, but it became even clearer for me one night when the "Options phone" rang at three in the morning. "Is this number just for women?" a male voice asked. By his tone, I could hear that he was drunk or high.

Is this a prank call? I wondered, but something kept me from hanging up. "No," I said, "the center is not just for women."

"My girlfriend just told me she's pregnant."

"What do you want her to do?" I asked.

"Well, she keeps telling me how she has her whole life planned out and how she can't have this baby," he said. "I'm not religious, but I know right from wrong. I'm young myself and I'm just not sure what to do."

"It sounds like you're medicating; it sounds like you're in emotional pain."

If there's one thing I learned, people drink alcohol or take drugs for a reason. It's not the drugs or the alcohol that's the problem—it's the pain causing them to want to numb, to medicate, to take away the pain through artificial means. Until the person deals with the pain, they will keep finding different ways to soothe it.

We pondered aloud how he could talk his girlfriend into coming into the center. I asked how long he had been using drugs and what the underlying reason was. That's when he shared. "I found out a while ago that I should have an older brother."

I heard a grimacing pain in his voice, and he took another drink. "I've always wondered what it would've been like to have an older brother; someone to watch out for me," he continued.

"What happened?"

I was unprepared for his answer. "My parents told me they aborted."

My eyes closed. Sometimes you never understand the ripple effect of your actions upon other people; you never understand how much what you do affects another person until you see it in someone else. I cannot describe the intense pain at that moment. I recalled the night Jodie and Lindsey said they always felt something was missing. The reality again of my abortion and its consequences hit me. I aborted my daughters' brother. I aborted my husband's namesake.

Before he said goodbye, the young man asked again for my name. "Can I call you again?" he asked.

"Of course," I responded.

I never heard from him again.

Another woman called the center on a weekend.

"Options Pregnancy Center, Melony speaking," I answered.

"Oh, I hoped no one would answer," a small voice said.

I knew the courage it took to make the call. She came in the next day to register for the next abortion recovery group. Her abortion took place thirty years earlier, at five months. Never had she attributed any problems to her abortion. She heard about the group through church and realized she had never dealt with it. Now she had grown children and grandchildren.

As each week of the group went by, I noticed changes in her. The spark that had been missing started to glow. She missed one week of the program and agreed to come in and catch up.

LIFE LESSON #25: *Writing about your feelings, then speaking them aloud are two different things. Writing about your feelings is like lancing a wound. Speaking about them lets the infection drain, relieving the pressure of what can be years of pent up emotion.*

Part of the healing process for a post-abortive woman involves finding a picture of what they sense the child may have looked like. Knowing that this was a human soul helps them focus. It was their child.

She said, "I can't find any picture that seems right. I keep envisioning a child in a neonatal unit or something like that. Can we skip this part?"

I searched for pictures and showed her.

"No," she said, "They're just not right."

I recalled a picture of a twenty-two-week old fetus, sucking its thumb in the safety of its mother's womb. I hesitated before showing her the picture. She gasped, "Oh no! No one told me. . . . No one told me. . . . If only I could undo what I've done!" she sobbed.

It is important to "be with" someone at that level of remorse and grief. The full gravity and weight of the abortion crashed onto her. She came face to face with the level of forgiveness God extended to her, and the degree of pain God asked His Son to endure to give forgiveness to her. And that He waited thirty years for that moment.

Once she finished grieving, she was able to be the wife, mother, and grandmother that God intended her to be from the beginning.

In December of 2008, a woman called. She said she had called the center five times and hung up each time. It took all of her willpower to walk through the door. She had no support, nothing. She had moved to the province, so she had no family or friends in the area. Two years earlier, she and her boyfriend placed a child for adoption. They did not heal from the pain. She was now thirty-five weeks pregnant with his second child, and the relationship was now in ruin. Alone and scared, she considered abortion.

After going through the options, she cried saying, "Okay I think I want to place this child for adoption." She asked if I would come to the ultrasound with her. I saw the baby's heart beating. I saw the nose, the lips, but most hauntingly of all, the eyes, wide open. The scripture, "I formed you in the secret place," from Psalm 139:15 took on a whole new meaning.

As we waited for baby to arrive, I was visiting my mom who lived eight hours away. The phone rang, it was the woman. "I wanted to make sure you were answering," she said, "Something might be happening."

Leaving at once, I reached the hospital at 2:30 a.m. to find her holding her baby daughter. The next day I brought gifts from the center that she could send with the baby, one being a white, soft blanket with pompoms on the end. She wrapped her baby in it, and for three days she didn't leave her side. I saw her every day. There was no one else to visit her. The baby went into foster care before she could pick adoptive parents. The most amazing foster mother picked up the baby. As the baby was placed in the car seat, her eyes did not leave her mother, gazing with the look a baby gives its mother when she knows something is happening, the "Mom? What's happening? Why are you crying?" look.

My heart broke. She kept the blanket to have something the baby used, something that had her scent, something to hold in the middle of the night when there was no baby to hold.

The door closed as the foster mother left the room. The baby was gone. She cried, and I held her. There were no words to say. She needed to be alone, so I drove her home.

My phone rang a few days later. "I'm not doing well. I'm so confused. Just tell me what to do, Mel, and I'll do it," she said.

"You know I can't do that." One of the toughest lessons I had learned was you can't "lead" someone to make a decision. It's their decision to make, not yours. You can, however, walk beside them as it's made.

She came in to the center to see me. "Part of me is missing, like I've lost my right arm." She named her child Abigail, and I gave her a Bible and highlighted the story of the woman her daughter was named after, hoping she would find comfort in His word. With a confidence I had never seen, she said, "I'm keeping her." The decision was made. Days later, she walked into the center, her daughter in her arms.

The next month, I received a call early in the morning. My mother was not doing well. Unexpectedly, her death seemed imminent. I flew around the house, quickly packing a bag, rushing to make the eight-hour drive, praying I would make it in time. Within ten miles from my house, the cell phone rang again. She was gone.

Driving out to the funeral, I realized the last time I saw her, I had been visiting and received the call from the woman giving birth—the woman who planned on placing her child for adoption, then didn't. Something was in all of that. I could not get my head around it.

On Mother's Day that year, there was no one to call. Oh, how I missed her and realized again how much I loved her. But that's not where the story ended. The woman and her boyfriend had tried to work things out. Again she became pregnant. Again they separated. "What am I going to do?!" she cried.

A week later, I tried to call, but the number was disconnected. I closed my eyes, positive she went for an abortion. I had seen this before. The pain of a woman placing her first child for adoption and not working through it, with no one supporting her, abortion seemed easier to bear.

Every few days I thought about her and her other child out there somewhere, alone. Days turned into weeks. Weeks turned into months, until I received a call one day. "Melony, there's a woman named Joanie on line two for you." I picked up the phone, but she hung up right away.

I sat there with my head in my hands. *She's aborted, and she's afraid to talk. She's afraid I will judge her,* I said chastising myself.

A few minutes later, the door opened. "Melony, Joanie is here to see you."

I ran up to the front and turned the corner. Abby was in her father's arms, Joanie standing there with a huge smile, holding a baby. "Hey Mel!" she said with tears flowing. "I want you to meet our son."

CHAPTER 25

The work at the center started taking its toll on our marriage. When I got home, I was extremely tired, and I was often speaking on evening and weekends. Lawrence started to hate the center. It was separating us more and more.

It became so bad that I alerted the board members as to what was happening. They knew they could not make decisions for me, so they prayed, and prayed.

It would be a couple of years before I realized that every time a fight broke out between Lawrence and me, I ran. Instead of facing what was happening, I would pack a bag and go to a hotel in the city or sleep on the couch at the center. It was becoming a familiar pattern.

Finally, I started doing what God had asked. I tried desperately to find balance and place Lawrence above the center. Our marriage started flourishing once again.

LIFE LESSON #26: When you start serving the Lord, the evil one will not be happy. Expect and be prepared for pushback.

CHAPTER 26

As part of my job as director, I contacted churches in the city, making them aware of the services the center provided. During one meeting, I met with a pastor's wife. Our hearts connected, and we shed many tears.

Previously, the center had fundraising banquets, and I felt led to have them again. I asked the pastor's wife to speak at the banquet on adoption since she and her husband had adopted their first daughter. A few months after the banquet, she asked me to be one of their "ministry partners." They partnered with various local, national, and international ministries and wanted to support the center.

One weekend per year, the partners came to their church so the congregation could learn more about the ministry partners the church supported. It would end with a Sunday service when the church members were asked to pledge support with prayers, volunteering, and finances.

The weekend came, and I had no idea what to expect. By the end, I was physically and emotionally exhausted, but more spiritually filled than I had been in a long while. During the weekend, I shared my story. One of the international partners, Ranji, a woman who ran an orphanage and school in Zambia, Africa, said, "Melony, you need to come and share your story in Africa."

During that weekend, she said it again. That same night, I sat in the audience with another one of the new local partners as the pastor interviewed the international ministry partners on stage. One of them was Ranji.

The Pastor said to Ranji, "I hear you and Melony Materi have been talking and you think she should go to Zambia and share her story."

"Yes, I'm really feeling strongly about this," Ranji replied.

I sank in my seat. The pastor looked right at me and said, "Melony, we will send you. Will you go?"

How many times had I prayed the prayer of Jabez, "Lord, I ask that you would bless me indeed and enlarge my territory. I ask that Your hand would be with me and that You would keep me from evil that I may not cause pain," from 1 Chronicles 4:10. But I did not consider Africa as part of my territory. And going there was not on my bucket list.

I don't remember my response. It was one of those "moments." I had no interest to go. But in my heart, it may as well have been Jesus Christ standing there asking. What was I going to say? No?

On the way home that night, I talked to God. "Lord, are You sure about this? Have you thought this through?"

Ranji spoke with me a few weeks later. "I'm hoping to set it up for you to speak to at least six hundred students in various schools," Ranji shared. "And there is one school the Department of Education keeps omitting from the list. I just keep insisting they put it back on." Whoever it was in the department had not yet learned that you don't say no to Ranji Chara.

Within a few months, the church made arrangements for another woman named Joanne, and myself to go. Before leaving, I googled various schools in Livingstone, Zambia, one school in particular came up, Linda High School. It indicated that the bright and more fortunate kids attended classes in the morning, with the less fortunate ones attending in the afternoon. I prayed it would be on Ranji's list to speak in the afternoon. I felt that something was to happen there. I didn't mention it to Ranji. She had enough on her plate. If God wanted me there, it would happen.

"Don't forget to watch out for the giraffes, dear," Ranji said to her husband as he drove us from the airport to their home in Africa. "It's that time of night."

I chuckled. Just like home, only different animals.

"Melony, here is the list of schools where you will be speaking. There will be more students than we thought. The total should be one thousand or more," she said calmly.

My mouth dropped. I looked at the list, and there it was— Linda High School.

Ranji prayed the students would react, and they did. At the end of each presentation, I gave them Ranji's cell phone number to call if they needed help. Calls started coming from girls who thought they might be pregnant.

An older man named Andrew, who worked for Ranji, drove us everywhere in a van. He was a very sweet man. One day as Andrew drove to the school, I asked him to stop at the graveyard. I'm not sure why I wanted to see it, but I felt compelled. I was not prepared. There were fresh graves as far as the eye could see with new ones being dug for the day. Death was constant.

Another morning, Ranji needed to stop at the store. Andrew

debated what to do. Go with Ranji or stay with Joanne and me? He decided to go into the store with Ranji, and we were given strict instructions to stay inside the van.

As we waited, an elderly, obviously very poor man, hobbled past the van. I looked at Joanne and said, "Do you want to give him some money?" We both felt prompted to. It was just one of those moments when if you don't do what you're being prompted to, you will regret it later.

We pooled some money together, and we devised a plan for one of us to give him the money while the other shielded so no one would see what we were doing. We were the only white people in the area. As if no one would notice! We watched him head down a back alley, stopping part way to go through some garbage, so we moved quickly to catch him.

A lot of young men were there. It wasn't safe. Joanne shielded while I approached him. His eyes darted back and forth. "My friend and I want you to have this money," I blurted, taking his hand and putting the money into it. His eyes pooled. It was as though I looked straight into the eyes of Jesus Christ.

A young man approached and asked for money. He must have seen us give the old man some cash. We were now afraid that the old man would be beaten up and robbed. How could we be so stupid?

We stood by the old man, guarding him, until he headed down the alley again, then we slowly backed out to the street, eyes on constant alert, watching to make sure no one tried to steal it from him. We also watched the young man who had asked us for money to make sure he didn't follow him.

Suddenly a healthy, clean, well-dressed man in his mid-twenties appeared behind us and said, "Don't worry, they have been informed to leave him alone. They will not take the money from him." When I looked around again, the man had vanished.

Joanne and I both looked at each other. "Was that an angel?" I said. Her eyes were as big as saucers as she nodded.

Another morning Ranji was doing business at the school. Joanne was working with the students, and I worked on emails. Ranji was informed that the mother of one of the boys that attended the school was there to take her child back to her home village. He was seven years old. The mother was asked when the child would be brought back. She said she didn't know. Ranji knew it meant only one thing. The mother was going home to die and had little time left.

Ranji started asking questions. The mother's lips quivered as her eyes swelled with tears. Ranji asked if anyone would educate the child in the village when she was gone. The mother didn't know. Ranji told her there was no room in the boys' home at the orphanage. She asked the mother to find someone in her village to take care of the child. If she couldn't, she was to come back that afternoon. I sat there, watching all of this take place.

Ranji went back to her paperwork. There was a knock on the door again. The principal of the school stood with another seven-year-old child. She had noticed the child wearing the same clothes for over a week. Her clothes were dirty and torn and her shoes too small. Ranji gently asked questions, the little girl's eyes wide like a deer in headlights. Her name was Anne. She was obviously traumatized. Ranji told the social worker to find out what was happening at the child's home. He came back to report the child lived with her older sister and the sister's boyfriend.

The school provided the children with clothing so the principal knew something was wrong when she saw the little girl in the same clothes every day. They found out that Anne's sister was selling the clothes the school provided for alcohol. Their home consisted of poles with the outside wrapped in plastic.

It was July, which meant it was winter, cold enough that we slept with the windows closed. The night before, I added an extra blanket onto my bed, and I thought about the little girl shivering in the middle of the night.

The social worker reported that Anne's sister had three children and Anne carried her sister's youngest baby around on her back. I noticed a young boy near one of the schools doing the same thing.

There was no doubt in Ranji's mind that Anne's sister and boyfriend were making Anne do all the cooking. Most likely, she would not be allowed to eat until the rest of them finished.

We prayed that Anne's sister would allow Anne to live at the Ebenezer School and were hoping she would sign the papers the next morning, but everyone realized that would mean losing her way of obtaining money for alcohol. Thankfully, Anne's sister agreed to have Ebenezer take the child in.

I asked Ranji if we could see where Anne lived, so that afternoon, we went to the ghetto. The Ebenezer van was familiar there with its tinted windows, but angry looking young men were trying to look inside. We held up a blanket so as not to be seen in the back. The people in the ghetto were wary of anyone taking pictures, possibly selling the pictures for profit.

Upon returning to the school, the mother who knew she was going to die soon was waiting. She could not find anyone to take her little boy. Ranji only had room for twelve boys. There were now seventeen, but she told her she would take the little boy in.

The mother stood there, her mouth quivering again, tears streaming, telling Ranji how grateful she was. Watching this scene, I numbed, memories floating through my mind of leaving Jodie in the hospital when I initially placed her for adoption, but that wouldn't compare to this.

I took a picture of her with her son. Ranji wanted it to give to the little boy one day in the future. The mother left knowing she would die. She would never see her son again.

When we left, the little boy sat by himself waiting to be taken to the orphanage. My heart broke. I came to understand more of how God wants to enter our suffering. I was grateful He allowed me to enter the suffering of the people there if only for a short time. Others could become God's hands and feet through what I had seen with my eyes and written with my hands.

Every time I presented at a school, two worship leaders played guitars and sang. Every time they did, my heart wanted to burst listening to all the children sing. They knew the words to every song. One day a girl asked if she could sing. She sang a cappella; a song about a broken heart and asking Jesus to take it, take it all.

Shame flooded my mind of thoughts I once had, that if someone was poor, abortion was okay. God convicted me, saying, "Why do you think your life is more precious to Me than theirs?"

The day came for the Linda High School presentation. I was pumped. My heart said that something major would happen. We arrived. We looked into the hall, then at each other in disbelief, then back into the hall. It was empty, except for one lone occupant that strutted around as though it owned the place, a rooster. I swear it looked at me and laughed. Ranji was on her phone immediately, her staff had confirmed and reconfirmed the dates and times.

"There's been a mix-up. The students are at the high school across the road. They've been waiting for over an hour!" she exclaimed.

"How can this be?" I was convinced something was to happen here, at this school.

The presentation went well, students shouting jubilantly as we got into the van. Once she took her seat, Ranji checked her phone. There was a text.

"My name is Lizzie. I'm 19 years old and in Grade 12. I got all the info on you people. I really need your help. I will explain everything to you only if you accept to help me. I have nowhere to turn. You are my last hope."

She called the number, and a girl answered.

"We are at Nansansu High School . . . oh . . . well do you live close to Linda High School? All right, we will meet you at the entrance to Linda High School in half an hour," Ranji said.

Half an hour later, she sat with us in our van, scared to death, at the entrance of Linda High School. "I already know your story. You spoke at our school the other day," she said shyly.

"Which school?" I asked.

When she named the school, it dawned on me that it was the one that kept being omitted from the list. "I recognize you. You were the girl with tears running down your face. You put your head down on your desk," I said gently.

"Yes," she said, tears streaming again.

I put my arm around her. The floodgates opened.

"I'm six months pregnant!" she wailed. "I live with my mother and stepfather. One of my stepsisters became pregnant and my stepfather kicked them out of the house! What am I going to do?"

"It is so obvious how much God cares for you Lizzie, and how much He cares for this baby," I said soothingly. "He has set up this whole thing. What are the chances of Ranji flying me half-way around the world to speak at your school?"

We consoled her, and held her. Ranji promised that if she was kicked out of her home, she would take her in at the orphanage and care for her. I glanced at Ranji. The orphanage was over-flowing. I was still learning to trust God.

"What were you going to do if we hadn't responded to your text?" Ranji asked.

"I had already made plans to kill myself."

We met one last time before I left. "You can do this Lizzie. God has plans."

Walking away, she kept looking back, hands shaking as she brushed away tears, mine shaking as I brushed away mine.

When I returned home, I was exhausted. I had shared with not just one thousand, but over two thousand kids. In Ranji's email updates, I learned that Ranji had visited Lizzie's home. It was a one-room shack with a sheet hung up to separate it into two rooms. Ranji and Lizzie told Lizzie's mother together. When her stepfather heard, he told Lizzie she had a week to get out. She was devastated.

Lizzie's stepfather was of a different faith. We prayed hard that he would change his mind about Lizzie. After three nights, he told his wife he was not sleeping well. Each night he had the same dream. Then he announced to his wife that God was telling him to care for Lizzie and her child. A few months later, Lizzie gave birth to a son.

LIFE LESSON #27: *You can't help everyone, but if you are obedient you can help those whom the Holy Spirit puts in your path.*

CHAPTER 27

The next year I attended training called "Genesis" at the same church that sent me to Africa. The training was based on Paul's teaching, "why do I do what I don't want to do?" For quite some time, God had been awakening a deeper root in me that needed healing. I had walked through the sexual abuse pain. I had walked through the abortion pain. But something else kept stirring. Was it adoption? With everything I had seen at the center as to how adoption affects the mother, why would it not affect the baby? I had no idea if adoption would come up, but a little voice inside me said it would.

The leader of the training taught about the limbic part of our brain and how memories are stored. However, the memories have no concept of time. Your limbic system knows you've read this book, but it has no idea if it was ten minutes ago or ten years ago. If a traumatic event occurred, your limbic system has no concept of when it happened.

If a person has a trauma in their past, decisions will filter through the trauma experience. Those trauma memories will be triggered, subconsciously reminding you of the event, causing you to react in certain ways, particularly with addictive behavior. Addictions enable you to soothe the pain, to numb yourself, rather than working through and responding appropriately. Addictive behaviors include not only alcohol and drugs; they can also be shopping, talking on the phone, technology, pornography, gambling, anything that will numb you and distract you from the pain of the traumatic experience that the trigger has caused. Unless you look at the trauma and figure out what your triggers are, you will continue to react instead of respond.

One morning, the leader talked about "attachment theory" and shared the work of John Bowlby. She showed pictures of a little monkey and experiments Bowlby initiated. Everyone thought the infant monkey would attach to the one who fed it, but the experiments showed otherwise. The baby monkey had a mother made of wire that gave milk and another mother made of wire and fake fur. The monkey would run for milk, and then run back to the "furry mother."

Then she said the words that penetrated my heart and met their mark, "the earlier the trauma, the more the effect."

She kept reiterating the statement. Tears welled from the deep root of trauma in my heart. I put up my hand. "Are you telling me that if a baby is placed for adoption, even within the first few days, it's considered trauma?" I asked.

"Yes, of course" she said.

I bolted from the room, running to the washroom. As tears streamed and with voice trembling, I asked, "God, where are you?" As I continued to weep, I turned, and there, scratched into the enamel of the soap dispenser, were the words, "I LOVE YOU."

I gasped. He had reached out, telling me He was with me and that everything would be okay. He showed me the truth. He wanted me to feel the pain and to be healed. But I could not heal if I did not admit that the wound was there.

LIFE LESSON #28: *You will not heal if you continue to deny that a wound exists.*

Later in the week I sat with the pastor of the church and told him what happened and how amazing the training had been.

"Let me tell you about my experience," he said. He spoke of the daughter he and his wife had adopted years earlier. They both loved her with all their heart. He knew a root of rejection would be present but he vowed to love it out of her. He vowed to tell her and show her every day how much he loved her. But the root of rejection reared its ugly head at two years of age.

"I picked up the pace and showed and told her even more, but it showed itself again when she was twelve years old. I felt as though I had failed as a father." My heart went out to this man, to my parents, and to all adoptive parents at that moment.

"I learned something important," he said. "You cannot love rejection or pain out of someone. You can walk beside them as they face it, but you cannot love it out of them."

I didn't realize then that his words were prophetic. I would recall them in a critical time in my life. And the words, "I LOVE

YOU" may have been scratched onto the soap dispenser, but I hadn't even scratched the surface of where God would lead me.

CHAPTER 28

God continued to use the center and continued to test my trust in Him. One day, a couple came in who were very scared. To them, abortion seemed to be their only way out. As we discussed all of their options, tears spilled down her cheeks. Her name was Susan, and her boyfriend, John, was visibly distraught.

"John, I have the utmost of respect for you for coming here today with Susan. I can see how much you want to protect her," I said.

When we finished talking, I asked if they would come back for a follow-up appointment. They did. I used to hold my breath for what seemed like an eternity until a couple came back, but I had learned to hand it over to God. Or so I thought.

They arrived for their second appointment, and John announced, "We've decided to have this baby."

My heart did a leap and I let out a breath. Jubilant and excited, they talked about how to tell their parents.

I kept in contact with Susan and John throughout the pregnancy. Everything was fine, but John called a week before the baby was to be born. "Susan is scared of the labor. The baby is seven pounds, eight ounces."

I told him to tell her not to worry, everything would be fine. A few days later, Sarah was born. Everything was not fine. "The baby and Susan both have an infection," John said. "Susan has to have surgery."

I held my breath again and sent out an urgent prayer request to the prayer chain. As the week went by, everything looked as though it would be okay, but by the end of the week, hopes were dashed. "The baby is okay but Susan is not." I could hear the desperation in John's voice. "She has to go in for surgery again."

Parents on both sides helped. John kept their baby, Sarah, with him at home and in the hospital, feeding her, changing her, loving her, and loving Susan. Susan was too weak to hold her precious new baby, but John would lay Sarah close beside her.

I will never forget the Saturday morning he called. "It doesn't look good. I don't know what will happen. What if I lose her? I have to be strong for her," he whispered.

"John?" I said, "You don't have to be strong when you're talking to me." He started to cry. I started to cry.

"God, you say that when two or three are gathered in your name, You are there. John and I pray that you heal Susan of whatever this is. We beg of you God."

The doctors gave Susan a one in five chance of making it through. After we hung up, this little voice nagged me. "You caused this. You talked them into having this baby," it accused.

"Oh, my God," I thought, "what have I done?"

Susan went through five surgeries. She was weak, but she and John came into the center the day after she got out of the hospital. John carried Sarah in her baby seat and assisted Susan.

"How are you Susan?" I asked. "You've been to hell and back. This place is the same as it was the first time you came in—it's safe."

The floodgates opened. All the emotions of the past weeks came gushing out. Both shaken by the experience, they knew it would be a long road to recovery. But they would make it.

We talked of the recent snowfall and what day it had occurred. John said, "It was Wednesday. I remember because I woke Sarah up so she could see it." Sarah was three weeks old.

I grinned. The mother in me thought, *you woke up a three-week old baby?* But the child in me thought, *John, you will be one awesome dad.*

"Well, I guess we should get going. She wants to do some shopping before we watch the game."

It was the way he said it that made me ask, "Who wants to go shopping before you watch the game?"

"Well, Sarah!" he exclaimed, as Susan giggled.

God taught me a huge lesson that day.

LIFE LESSON #29: *If God moves in a situation, He will do so whether we hold our breath or not. He never asks us to sit and hold our breath. He asks us to pray.*

Another woman came into the center who had aborted her child thirty years earlier. She was ready to walk through the pain of that fateful decision.

One reason women who have had abortions need to stay in denial is to escape facing the fact that they are the mother of their unborn child—their aborted child. Staying in denial helps us to not look at the pain. God gave women the natural desire to nurture and protect their babies, not to hurt them.

But a woman learns how to be a mother from her mother. I read somewhere that we form our self-worth through our mothers and our identity from our fathers. And sometimes a woman has to learn how to protect her child from her own mother.

She told me she was sexually molested by her father many times. She said she had forgiven him. When I asked about her mother, she said, "My mother was good to me."

"Can you tell me more?" I asked. "Where was your mother when this was happening?"

She cried softly at first, quickly escalating to uncontrollable sobbing. Years of pain spilled out. "My mom was sitting right there the first time he touched me and she did nothing."

Tears streamed down my face. I said nothing. I didn't have to. After a time of silence, I said, "God loves you."

She had trouble thinking anyone loved her, let alone God. I asked her if she had any paper money. She didn't, and neither did I. I drew up a fictitious one-hundred-dollar bill and asked her to pretend it was real. I asked her if she had given the money its value. She said no. I asked if I had. "No," she said, "you didn't either." She agreed something greater had given its value.

"Would you like to have the money?"

"Of course!" she exclaimed.

I took the money and crumpled it, asking if she would still like to have it. It didn't look so nice now. She still wanted it.

Taking the money, I spit on it and threw it to the ground, stomping on it.

"Would you still like to have it?"

"Yes!" she exclaimed again.

Looking her in the eye, I said, "This is the way God views you. No matter what has happened to you or what you've done, you are still worth your same original value to God. And He always wants you back."

Tears formed in her eyes. "Why?" she cried out. "Why does He love me?"

I gazed at her, my own tears flowing again and said, "I don't know why He loves you or why He loves me. All I know is He does."

I started to throw the fictitious money into the garbage, but she asked me if she could keep it. I will never forget what she did next. She took the pretend money and quietly put it into her purse.

LIFE LESSON #30: God's love for us never changes. He loves us the same as yesterday, the same as today, and He will love us the same tomorrow, no matter what has happened.

One woman was brought in by her friend. She was hesitant to proceed with the pregnancy, and I wasn't sure which choice she would make. After we met, her friend called two days later. "She's decided to have the baby, and she asked to see you again!" I thanked God, knowing what was in store if she chose the other option.

Each time I saw her, I encouraged her. One day her mother called. She told me some complications arose, and the baby would not survive. The doctors advised her to abort, but she chose to trust. She chose to honor what was entrusted to her.

Two days later the phone rang again. She had lost the baby at twenty weeks. I made a trip to the hospital to visit her. The hospital room door was closed, so I opened it slowly. Everyone had left. She was lying in bed, alone. She looked at me then gazed off into space. Her face looked blank. She showed no emotion. Sitting on her bed, I never said a word.

"Why did this happen?" she whispered. "After he was born, we held him. He was so small he fit into the palm of my hand. I watched him take his last breath. I held him as he died. I prayed for God to save him. But He didn't listen! Where was He?" she wailed.

"God cares. He is here right now. I wish I could give you the answers," I said, "I wish I could tell you why this happened, but I can't. If I could take this pain away from you, I would."

"People are telling me I will have other children," she said numbly.

I knew that she would have to move through this pain or risk becoming stuck. Then she would start avoiding it and start stuffing it down. It would infect her, and everyone around her.

"People mean well when telling you that. No one likes to see other's cry, but tears are there for a reason. People don't realize that when they say that, it takes away from the honor and dignity of the child. It's like saying if something happened to your mom, it's okay because you'd be able to get another one. Nothing will replace this person. Nothing will replace this child."

Her pain broke through. She cried relentlessly. Her wails filled the room.

Oh God, I thought to myself. *Please help her Lord; tell me what to say; show me what to do.* My heart was breaking for her. My own tears spilled. "Can I hold you?" I asked.

"Yes!" she cried.

I sat on the bed and held her close, rocking her, but it wasn't me who held her that day. It was Jesus Christ. He says He will never leave us nor forsake us. He asked me to keep my lips closed and to hold her and be with her. Her heart was breaking, and He was there.

One young woman had been in and out of youth facilities since she was twelve. And now she was in another one. "I'm pregnant," she said on the phone, "and I'm not sure what to do."

She decided to keep her baby. I called her off and on to see how she was doing. Then she was transferred somewhere closer, and I could see her more frequently. I learned that she had a traumatic childhood, and we talked about working out the pain in her life so it would stop affecting her life and not filter through to her child.

One day I brought "the blocks" with me. Sixteen blocks fit snugly into a box. God had given me the idea, and I used them when presenting in classrooms and with people who came into the center.

This woman knew of my pain and how it had infected me and those around me. I handed her the box and said, "This box of blocks represents your life. I want you to envision pain in your life that you haven't worked through, something you haven't talked about. Now I want you to hand me the number of blocks that pain represents."

She handed over blocks, one, two, three, four, and five. A look of resignation settled in her eyes. With tears, she handed me the whole box.

"That's a lot of pain." I put the blocks back in the box and handed it to her. "You've been trying to work through the pain yourself. How's that working for you?"

She looked down. "Not well—not well at all."

I took an extra block and said, "This block represents love I would like to give to you. I want you to try to fit it into your box." It wouldn't fit.

"What's wrong?" I asked.

She looked at me, tears flowing and said, "It won't fit. There isn't enough room."

"I see," I said, "I wonder, how you will give love to others? And how are you going to give love to your child when you can't accept any yourself?"

I grabbed another box of blocks. This one had sixteen gold blocks. They glistened and reflected the light in the room as I opened them.

"What if you handed the pain over to something far bigger and greater than yourself, something able to handle it?" I asked. Then I asked her to take one block out of her box. She looked at them for a while. The pain had taken root and settled in her years before. Was she ready to let go?

She slowly removed a block and handed it to me. I took one of the gold blocks and handed it to her. "Will this gold block fit into your box now?"

"Yeah, it will" she said.

"Hmmmmm, and your blocks of pain fit perfectly into this box," I said, pointing to the box with golden blocks. "This box of gold blocks represents God," I told her, "and He can give you far more love than I or anyone could ever give you. But you have to hand your pain over to Him."

It was time to leave, so I put everything away. She was holding the gold block. She twisted it around in her hand as though it were something she might have seen before but had lost. "Melony? Do you think I could keep this block?"

"Yes," I said, "you can keep it. There are enough gold blocks for everyone."

During a classroom presentation one day, when one of the participants realized my "love block" would not fit into their box of blocks because there wasn't enough room, he said, "So you make a bigger box . . ." I told him what he said was profound. The government was talking about initiating a research program into why obesity was becoming so prevalent. It was clear what's needed is for people to work through their pain; otherwise they continue to make a "bigger box" to fit it in.

LIFE LESSON #31: You may have had a childhood experience that subconsciously tells you there is not enough to go around, but God has enough love for everyone. And He has enough love for you.

CHAPTER 29

One day, I had a speaking engagement in a high school classroom. I had spoken to hundreds of kids during classroom presentations, but the school I was about to speak in was different. Not only was it the first *public* high school I would speak in, it was my old high school, the school I attended when we moved to the city from the farm after I gave birth to Jodie—the school I felt swallowed up in.

The teacher told them a little about what I would share, so they appeared guarded.

I told them about being sexually molested as a child, being pregnant at fifteen and choosing to keep my child, and having another child at twenty-two. Then I started talking about the abortion at twenty-three and that I had made the wrong choice.

"You shouldn't be saying your abortion was a bad choice," a young man blurted.

"I understand what you're saying" I said, "but why don't you wait until I've finished and see if your thoughts are the same." I continued to share how life became infected with pain, so much so it oozed out and affected those around me.

I shared about the adoption and of the emotional pain my birth mother endured. "So I hope you're seeing pain was involved for the mother no matter what choice she makes, whether its adoption or abortion, but there's one difference." They looked intently as I raised my hand and said, "I'm here."

Shock displayed itself on their faces as they were shown the number of abortions per year versus the number of adoptions per year in the province.

"My aunt and uncle have been trying to adopt a baby," someone said. It was the same young man who said abortion wasn't a bad choice. "They've been waiting for years," he said. "Why does it take so long?"

I looked at him, turned back to the screen and the high number of abortions compared with the lower number of adoptions, then turned back to him. "Why do you think?" I asked very softly. His eyes turned down.

At the end, I asked if anyone would be offended if I used the word "God." No one said a word. Using the same money analogy I always used at the center, I asked, "Does someone have a twenty dollar bill I can use for the demonstration?"

"I've got one!" a voice piped. It was him again.

I asked the class if they wanted it. "Yes!" they shouted.

The motions of spitting, throwing it to the ground, and

stepping on it had become so familiar as I related it to how God sees our value and that He always wants us back no matter what our condition.

When finished, I told the young man I would give him a clean twenty-dollar bill. "That's okay," he said, "I'd like to keep this one."

The next day, I started to cry when I read his evaluation form. "I would recommend this presentation to any class. She really opened up my mind on abortions and all the problems that come with having one. I really enjoyed Melony's presentation. It was amazing."

A few months later, he shared at our fundraising banquet that his opinion on abortion has totally changed.

PART V

Honor Your Father and Mother

CHAPTER 30

During the summer of 2011, Lawrence and I arrived at a small town, our destination for the day. But this wasn't just any town. And this wasn't just any destination.

We arrived early. When Lawrence had heard the name of the town, he said his parents used to make the day-long trip once per year to visit relatives there. He wanted to see if anyone with the Materi name was buried in the cemetery.

The church was easy to find, the cemetery located behind it. A woman was tending the yard and asked if we would like to go into the church to look at the cemetery map. "Are you just travelling through?" she asked as we followed her to the church.

"No we're here visiting someone," Lawrence quickly answered protectively as he glanced at me.

We walked inside and stood in awe. The sanctuary was breathtaking. Lawrence looked at the cemetery map, but my feet took me to the sanctuary. I could sense God's presence. "Well, here we are God, just You and me," I whispered. "I have no idea what You're about to do, but I know You will be right here with me."

A few months earlier my daily scripture reading made me very uncomfortable. The reading for the day included the commandment, "Honor your father and mother, that your days may be long upon the land which the Lord your God is giving you," Exodus 20:12.

I remember closing my eyes. This was a place I had not wanted to go. Over the next few days, it kept bothering me. I knew the feeling wasn't referring to my adoptive mom and dad, or my birth mother. I had honored them every time I shared my story and in so many other ways. It referred to my birth father—someone I never spoke of.

The picture my birth mother painted of him in the letters she left for me was not a nice one. *Why would I want to honor someone like that?* I thought to myself. The answer came right away, "Because if not for this man, you would not exist. I'm asking you to honor him. I'm asking you to trust Me."

Aware of how adoption affected birth parents, I felt God wanted me to find my birth father. If he was struggling, he would have a sense of peace before he died. This had nothing to do with me. I would do this for him.

No doubt, God chuckled to Himself, saying, "If you think I'm having you do this just for him, you tell yourself whatever you need to tell yourself, my dear."

Back home, I went through the process of finding him, not knowing his name. "Something came for you in the mail" Lawrence said. I had sent in the paperwork to access all of my adoption papers which included papers from Social Services. They had arrived.

Hours went by, but the package sat unopened. "Aren't you going to open it?" Lawrence asked.

There was a real chance my identity, the surname I was supposed to have, would be written somewhere on those documents. And I would open it when I was ready.

When I did finally find the courage to open the package, there were several papers to look through. I searched for his name, unable to find it.

"It's not here! Where is it?" I exclaimed, quickly scanning each page again.

Suddenly, there it was, in black and white. I gasped. "I have a father," I whispered, "and here is his name." His first name was Peter. Tears fell, and I realized for the first time in my life I was supposed to be here. And this man was a real person, with real feelings.

But there was something else written in the papers. He had denied paternity. I felt like someone had shot an arrow into my heart. I controlled the feeling, put it in a box in my heart and attached a "Do Not Enter" sign on it.

I spoke with a friend of the turmoil, sharing how God was asking me to honor this man. "But how do I do that?" I asked her. "Can't I honor him by praying for him? Do I have to contact him? Can't I honor him without doing that?"

Twenty years earlier, I mourned the death of the ghostly image of the birth mother I never got to meet. Did I have the strength to go through it again if he too had passed away? But most important, I did not want to hurt my dad. I would rather die.

My friend pondered everything I said. It seemed an eternity before she spoke. "Maybe you should ask for your dad's blessing before contacting your birth father," she said.

It was a good idea, so I prayed and went to visit my dad. I told him how much I loved him; about the psychological connection between our Heavenly Father and our earthly father; about how I see young people at the center every day who have major issues both emotionally and spiritually because of not feeling loved by their fathers; about how I've recognized how much he has loved me unconditionally my whole life and that I've been able to trust God more and more because of it. Finally, I shared the incredible things happening at the center.

With tears he said, "Apparently you were supposed to be on this earth."

I looked at him with tears and said, "And apparently you were supposed to be my dad."

I asked for his blessing to contact my birth father, and he gave it.

I tried to prepare myself emotionally before starting the contacting process. Lawrence kept telling me, "He will be really happy to see you!" And I kept responding, "No, I don't think he will be happy." But in the end, I had to go where God was leading.

I Googled his name, and there was one only person with that name in the whole country. My adoption papers indicated his faith denomination was Catholic, so I asked the priest in the area to make the initial contact.

The priest had done nothing like this before. Upon satisfying himself that this was the right man, he went to see him. "What does she want?" Peter asked him guardedly.

"She wants you to know she's okay," he said, "and she wants you to be okay too."

The priest called me at the center. An abortion-minded client was arriving within minutes. "Melony, I've spoken with him. He wants to have contact with you."

I closed my eyes. A sigh of relief escaped my lips.

"He wants to see you as soon as he can. And he wants your phone number. He wants to call you tonight." I wasn't comfortable with Peter having my phone number. I would call *him*. I needed to be the one in control.

That night, I made the call and heard his voice for the first time, the man whose DNA I shared but had never laid eyes on. I was never afraid to show my emotions, yet there I sat talking to him in complete control, emotionless. Lawrence sat in the chair next to me, always someone in control of his emotions, yet there he sat, weeping.

I asked Lawrence afterward why he wept. "I know how much this has affected your whole life," he said. "I've been thinking a lot about all of this and I've tried to imagine what it would be like to not know my roots . . . to not know where I came from . . . to not know and feel my identity."

We made arrangements to meet Peter in a few weeks. After visiting the cemetery again and meeting with God in the sanctuary, we walked up to the door of Peter's home, everyone nervous. We awkwardly hugged each other, and he introduced his wife. We sat at the kitchen table, and I found it difficult not to stare at him and study his features.

He told me he was just entering carpentry school when he learned that Pearl, my birth mother, was pregnant. A family member told him this could be anyone's child and that he should just forget her. He took the family member's advice.

After a while he took me into their living room and showed me pictures of his brothers and sisters, and his wife's children. He had no children of his own. Then he showed me his wedding picture. "I didn't marry until later in life after what happened," he said.

"What are you referring to?"

"Your birth," He explained how deeply it affected him, sometimes destructively. "I have felt my whole life as though something has been missing," he said. "I've missed the graduations, the weddings, I've missed it all." His eyes started to glaze over. "But now that I've met you, I have such a sense of peace."

I started to cry. He hugged me and said, "I'm sorry, I didn't mean to make you cry."

"Oh no!" I exclaimed. "These are not tears of pain." I explained that through working at the center I came to understand the pain that both women and men endure when they place a child for adoption; the sense of loss, loneliness, regret. And just as with other pain, they do everything they can to mask it. I knew the pain my birth mother felt because of what she wrote in her letters, and I felt I caused it.

But when it came to him, my birth father, I didn't think he had any pain. And if he did, I didn't think I was worth it. It was a paradox. I didn't think I was worth *his* pain. I was wrong.

Over the next few months, he called and left messages. Lawrence repeatedly asked me if I would return the call, and I told him I would call him soon. Lawrence always gave me a quizzical look. I could not explain the feelings that rose in me. All I knew was that I had them.

In November of the same year, I had driven out to see Dad for his birthday. I spent one night with Peter and his wife on the way back. They had kept asking me to come and visit.

That night, I met some of Peter's brothers and sisters. One of his sisters asked where Dad lived. Peter said, "That's her adopted dad. But now we've found each other. I'm her real dad."

Anger rose in me from a deep, deep place in my spirit. But my face did not reflect it. God says He is the potter and we are the clay. I could sense Him digging His thumbs into me, touching areas of my emotions I hadn't known were there.

Peter kept calling. He told me he loved me and I politely said it back.

CHAPTER 31

In February of 2012, I was to give the Sunday message at one of the churches that supported the center. I knew God was asking me to share about adoption pain. Fear gripped my heart. I knew He wanted me to talk about the "three mountains" in my life—sexual abuse, abortion, and adoption. I knew people would understand the first two mountains, but I did not think they would understand the third. But as Richard Uhrlaub says, "Adoptees need words to help navigate what in important respects is a dual reality. She or he is simultaneously: a social problem and a precious gift; a symbol of shame and normative family; a source of grief and joy; a human being and a commodity; the answer to one mother's prayers and an alleged threat to another mother's privacy . . ."* As the date drew closer, I felt a familiar pushing sensation—a nudge from God.

That Sunday, I shared all I felt God asking me to share, and I cried with the emotion. At the end, I did something I had never done before. I talked of earlier distrust in my life, especially of God. Randomly picking a man from the congregation, I asked him to help me with a demonstration. Blindfolding myself, I went to the back of the stage, asking him to use his voice to guide me off the stage and down the steps.

The man told me how many steps to take this way and that, to avoid objects on the stage. I asked how much further I had until the stairs started. He said about three feet. He told me to keep listening to the sound of his voice. He asked me to reach out for his hand two feet away. I flailed until I found it, grabbing it tightly as he talked me down the stairs. Applause resounded as I reached the bottom. I took off my blindfold and gave him a big hug. It was the perfect demonstration of my trust in God and following His voice blindly.

That's when Satan started in on me. All the way home I kept questioning the things I had said, even though people told me how touched they were. The next morning, Lawrence said I had been whimpering in the middle of the night as I slept.

As I drove in to the center that morning, my mind bombarded me with accusations that I had placed stumbling blocks in people's way instead of helping to remove them. I prayed aloud and asked God to give me confirmation that I had done the right thing by exposing the pain I had felt about adoption. After I got to the office, I received a text from a friend. She said

---

*Richard Uhrlaub, see http://secretsonsanddaughters.org/ssd/

she heard the presentation had gone well. I texted her back and said Satan had been taunting me about it all morning.

She texted me back and said, "This is what I know. The man who guided you down the steps had supper with us last night. He went on and on about how amazing the presentation was. They said there wasn't a dry eye in the house and that it was just awesome."

I phoned her. "You have no idea how much God just used you!" I told her I had prayed that God would give me confirmation that I had done the right thing and here she was telling me that the man, whom I had never met before, that I had randomly picked from the audience to represent God, had told her he thought it was awesome!

I had asked God for confirmation. And I got it.

CHAPTER 32

Just before I met Peter, my biological father, he had been diagnosed as cancer-free after a fight with bowel cancer. But it was back. "The doctor says he has one year to live, Melony," his wife unloaded as she called one day on the phone.

This emotional roller-coaster was almost too much to bear. I wanted to get off. I walked into his hospital room two days later. One of his sisters and her husband were there. As soon as Peter's eyes met mine, we both wept. How could this be happening now? My heart spilled over with compassion.

I spoke with him every couple of days on the phone. He was raised as a Catholic but had not attended church for a long time. I asked him if he would like for me to arrange for a priest to come and give him the sacrament of the Anointing of the Sick. He said he would.

I made the arrangements for Sunday. He called back two days later to say he wanted to cancel it. I wanted to do something for him, and I felt denied, again. Anger welled in me. He asked if I would still come and see him that Sunday, and I said I had other things planned. I could hear his disappointment as he breathed into the phone. But just as before, each time that I felt anger rise, I asked God to wash me with His grace.

I awoke that cold, blustery Sunday morning with a start. And I did not appreciate what God was asking me to do. I felt Him asking *me* to anoint Peter and pray for him.

I argued with God, telling Him it was not a nice day and that I would much rather go to church and then spend the afternoon with Lawrence in front of the fire with a nice glass of wine. My argument was met with deaf ears. And grace.

That afternoon, I walked into the hospital room with my anointing oil. It was the first time we had been alone. Baseball was one of his passions. There was a game on the small television. I was thankful for it. It helped to fill the awkward moments.

We spent hours sharing what happened in each other's lives. I told him everything; the good, the bad, and the ugly. I cried. He cried. He told me about the other passion in his life, alcohol. It almost destroyed him. Even up to two years before, someone would find him passed out in the back alley.

His remorse was almost palpable. His eyes filled with tears once again as he told me how much he loved me and how sorry he was. I knew he was saying he was sorry for not fulfilling his role as a father.

In that moment, I sensed it was time. I dripped oil onto my fingertips and slowly made the sign of the cross on his forehead and on each of his hands. He gazed, skeptical yet hopeful, into my eyes as I prayed, "In the name of the Father, and of the Son, and of the Holy Spirit."

In that instant, his body did not heal, but his spirit did.

He asked if he could give me something.

"Peter, that's not what this, is about. I want nothing from you." But I changed my mind. "I do want something," I said, my eyes lowering away from his.

"Anything," he responded.

"I want the hammer you used the most when you were a carpenter." I do not understand why I asked for it. Why would I want it?

"It's in my shed. But I can't give it to you," he said softly. "It's broken."

"I don't care if it's broken, I want it anyway."

"Ok . . . I'll make sure you get it," he said hesitantly.

Two weeks later, I heard a message about God not allowing us to minister to others until we have learned to love those closest to us. The next morning as I drove into work, I pondered the message. I knew God was not just asking me to honor my father, He was asking me to love him. I wrestled with God, again.

All the memories bombarded me. Opening my adoption papers and seeing his name for the first time; the stabbing in my heart when I read he had denied paternity; the anger that rose when he said we found each other and that he was my real dad.

Thoughts poured into my head. *No, I found you. You never came looking for me, and when my birth mother was pregnant with me, you denied being my father, remember?*

More memories flooded. The anger finding out Pearl had died six months before I found her. The anger knowing she had been looking for me but I never got to spend time with her. How ironic that Peter was the one I came to know!

The anger continued to rise until it broke through any grace or mercy I felt toward him. I became enraged. I yelled out in my car, "Give me a break God! How can You ask me to honor this man? How can You ask me to love this man who didn't even want to be my father! NO, NO, NO!" I screamed at the top of my lungs.

Upon returning home from the center that day, I vented more. The anger slowly dissipated like air escaping from a tiny hole in a big balloon. Finally, it appeared to leave.

At 3:30 that morning, the phone rang. Peter had died. Shock waves rolled against my heart. How could this be? He was supposed to live for a year. It had only been two and a half weeks.

The tears for Peter's life fell as Lawrence and I prayed. I praised God and thanked Him for his life. He was the vessel God chose to be my father. In the beginning, he may have denied me, but it did not change that he was my father. The journey was hard, but I had honored him. There was no higher honor I could have given him. I was thankful for finding him, for the timing and for the sense of peace he had before he died.

Jodie and Lindsey said, "Mom, you are at peace now. And so is he."

CHAPTER 33

That night I shared my story at a banquet in the same city we lived in when I aborted. Peter had died at 3:30 that morning, and I honored him as I shared that night.

A week later was his memorial. I decided to attend it by myself. As I drove, my body wanted to curl up into the fetal position. The closer I got, the worse I felt.

I spoke at the memorial, and there wasn't a dry eye in the house. Afterward, so many people wanted to talk. But there was one person I will never forget. He was an older gentleman who had also been adopted. He asked me how I went about finding my birth father. He stood there with tears, clearly thinking of the prospect of finding his own birth father. "I'm so scared," he whispered.

On the outside, stood a mature man, on the inside, a trembling little boy cringed at the thought of what he might find. Memories flooded my mind of how scared I had been when I started the adoption journey. A vision popped into my head of the two of us as little children, me putting my arm around him and telling him everything would be okay.

After the funeral, Peter's stepsons and his wife took me back to their home. They handed me the only thing I had asked for, his hammer. It was indeed broken.

CHAPTER 34

Just before Mother's Day of 2012, shortly after Peter died, I sent out a prayer email. In it, I spoke of the pain triggered in some adoptees that came into the center when they contemplated the approach of Mother's Day. I received a response to the email from an adoptive mom. She said, "I am relieved to read that some adopted children don't have good relationships with their adoptive moms. Maybe there's not much wrong with me after all."

Mother's Day was stressful for her. She had spent years wondering why she was so "unspecial." It never occurred to her that her adopted children may have not been looking forward to Mother's Day either.

I bought flowers and showed up on her doorstep the next

day. I attached a card that read, "From an adoptee to an adoptive mom. There is nothing wrong with you. God loves you. And so do I."

It had been three years since Mom passed away. On Mother's Day, I took flowers to her grave. She tried to love me when I was little but I didn't accept her love. After a while, I think she just gave up trying. Oh, how I wish I could've explained it to her now. Looking at the stone on her grave, I pulled away the weeds and grass from it. When reflecting later, I knew that as the weeds were pulled, the seed of rejection planted in me when I was born was spiritually uprooted. Weeping, I replaced the weeds and grass with a dozen red roses.

That night, a group of birth mothers held a "Journey of Healing" service after going through the birth mother support program. Dianne, the Birth Parent Support volunteer at the center had led them through their pain. She placed her first son for adoption and understood the impact it had on her own life. I read a letter to my birth mother after they read letters to their children placed for adoption. The truth set us free.

Women and men continued to come into the center. One day a woman came in who had three abortions. She wanted to abort the child she was now carrying. Too far along to abort even in the adjacent province, if someone could perform it elsewhere in the country, she still wanted to abort.

When I asked her where she was on the scale, (one being aborting and ten being having the child), she adamantly said, "One! And it won't be a problem to scrape together enough money to have an abortion, wherever I can get one!"

She had suffered a traumatic experience with her father as a child, and it was evident she had not emotionally healed. You could almost feel his ghost in the room, still haunting her. She was beyond angry and bitter about the experience, rage trying to escape through every pore of her body.

After viewing pictures of fetal development and explaining how an abortion was performed, she matter-of-factly said, "Yes, that's fine." After educating her on adoption and talking of my own adoption, she said, "I would never give someone else this curse."

"I hope one day you can work through that because by what you said, you've told me I was a curse."

Using the blocks, I asked her to think of a painful experience, knowing the childhood experience caused huge trauma. "The only painful experience I can think of is that I can't find an abortion clinic to get rid of this child." So, we used the blocks for that.

When the love block was held out to her, I asked if she could fit it into her box. The rage melted as the root started to expose itself. Pools of tears formed in her eyes. "It won't fit," she said. "There isn't any room for love."

"I have a feeling your childhood experience caused tremendous pain. Whenever it's brought up, your eyes glaze over and you try not to cry."

She broke down, and I told her I could refer her to a counsellor to help her walk through the trauma. "I don't trust counsellors," she replied.

"Do you trust me?" I asked.

She paused. "I don't know you well and you haven't screwed me over yet."

"I'm not here to screw you over. No matter what, I'll be here for you."

After an hour of talking, she appeared to be mentally reconstructing the walls that had fallen. When she left, I asked if I could give her a hug. I was shocked by the response. She held on and was not letting go. "I can't believe you want to hug me. No one has ever hugged me like that," she whispered.

I asked her if she wanted another one. She did.

A few months went by. I tried to contact her to no avail. My heart sank thinking of her. Had she scraped together enough money to have the abortion elsewhere?

Months later, my co-worker came into my office. Someone was there to see me. It was her. She smiled as she stood there, holding a baby.

CHAPTER 35

In 2010 another "door" opened. As my best friend Kate and I prayed, I told her I felt that one day I would speak in a prison. Undoubtedly, there would be post-abortive women there. "Really?" she said. "I can get you in."

It wasn't long before we made semi-annual trips to the women's prison in the province. On one visit, we heard something after parking our motorbikes in the parking lot.

Tap tap tap . . . tap tap tap.

As usual, we were being watched, but this time it wasn't just by the guard manning the security camera. We could sense other eyes peering at us. We heard the sound again.

Tap tap tap . . . tap tap tap.

The source of the sound was a few of the inmates waving frantically and tapping on the heavily barred windows, trying to get our attention. They were excited to see us. We smiled and waved back.

The chaplain signed us in, and the main prison door closed. A shiver went up my spine hearing the sound of metal against metal. It is a sound I never get used to.

The chaplain always invited us to eat with "her girls." We did not take this lightly. We went there to share about ourselves, to share how Christ had moved in our lives. It was important for us to "break bread" with them.

The "girls" always looked so normal. I expected them to look tough, hardened, but they looked like anyone on the street. They could be your sister, or an aunt, or your mother. I already knew it didn't matter where you came from, or what your race, color creed, religion, or economic status was—women are women, and pain is no respecter of persons.

And yet, I remembered our first time at the prison thinking, "How on earth am I going to relate to *these* women?"

The feeling wavered upon sharing with them. The sexual abuse, the teen pregnancy, almost giving my baby away, the divorce, the remarriage—the prison I had built for myself. I could still hear and feel the prison door closing on my soul. I could hear the guard throw the key away when I had the abortion. Tears streamed down their faces.

I hesitated and said, "I took the life of my child. If anyone should be in this prison; if anyone should be in this place, it's me." The relationship was sealed. We were all in there together— fellow inmates.

I shared about the guilt and shame that had been so deeply embedded in me. I shared how I didn't think God would ever want to have anything to do with someone like me, but He sent His only son to die for me, to die a horrible death in my stead. He opened the gate to the personal hell I had placed myself in and He threw away the key so far no would ever be able to find it again. And now He lifted my chin and filled my soul with a love that outshone the sun.

Every time we went to the prison and every time we shared, you could hear the spiritual chains of the women rattling.

CHAPTER 36

I saw it in almost every woman that came into the center, whether it was someone coming in for a pregnancy test, someone pregnant and abortion-minded, someone who had placed a child for adoption, or someone who experienced abortion. The seed of understanding planted a few months earlier, took root. God had been speaking about "father pain."

A new post-abortive client had three abortions. She was in major pain. All three abortions occurred within a short time. It was clear she repeatedly subconsciously tried to replace what was lost.

The fact that she'd had an abusive father explained the attraction to abusive boyfriends. After explaining "father pain," she understood. It was obvious she had been trying her whole life to get the love she never received from her father from other men. So much so, she chose men just like him. She would do anything to hear the words, "I love you."

God had been repeatedly putting this issue in front of me. When I tried to avoid it, He plunked it in front of me again. With each pregnancy, this woman could not see the value of her own children. Was it because her father did not see *her* value?

She did not believe in God. That made perfect sense. Why would she believe in a spiritual Father when her earthly father treated her with such disdain? Over and over, the subconscious earthly/spiritual father connection presented itself. If the person had a faith, I asked if they trusted God. They always said yes, but they learned that wasn't so.

Did they think God would protect them? The response was no. Did their earthly father protect them? No. Did they think God would provide for them? No. Did their earthly father provide for them? No. Did they think God would be there for them? No. Were their earthly fathers there for them? No.

After speaking with her for a while, I asked if she wanted to participate in the post-abortive program. She immediately said, "Yes." I asked her if she was okay with the program being Biblically based. She was. She didn't know how to use a Bible and asked how to pronounce the word "Psalm" when she saw it. I prayed His Word and the Psalms would come to mean the world to her.

It was obvious her father had pain in his own life; otherwise he would not have treated his own daughter that way. It was important that *she* come to that realization, so that one day she could forgive.

CHAPTER 37

In July of 2012, just three months after he died, my anger toward Peter flared up again. I chopped, sliced, and diced things for supper that night. Lawrence heard my chopping and came into the kitchen. "What's the matter?" he asked.

"My anger has risen, once again."

"The man is dead, Melony."

"I don't care! There was no excuse! He was twenty-five years old when I was born!" I grabbed the hammer. "Every time I look at this I want to scream! I hope it was worth it, Peter. You gave me up for this!"

By this point in life, I understood that when I did something in the "physical realm," something would happen in the "spiritual realm." (A good example is being baptized. Something physical is happening but something spiritual occurs.)

I had to do *something*. Ridding myself of the anger once and for all was necessary, otherwise a firm root of bitterness would be established. The idea of a ceremony came to mind. Off and on, I wore a necklace with a stone heart. It needed to be part of the plan.

My plan in place, I chose a Sunday in August—the birthday of my birth mother. With pictures of Peter and Pearl, a brick, Peter's hammer, and the stone heart from the necklace, I headed out to the yard. I told Lawrence I would let him know when the ceremony was complete.

If not for the people in the pictures, I would not exist. I spoke with Peter and Pearl as though they were right there, and I also conversed with God, praying fervently.

Placing the stone heart on the brick, I prayed for God to break the hearts of the fathers who wanted nothing to do with their children. I knew it was the key. But God turned the key back on me. As I raised Peter's hammer to break the stone heart, God spoke to my heart, saying, "Melony, it's YOUR stony heart that needs to be broken." I put the hammer down. Raising it again, I slammed it on the heart. Parts flew in different directions, leaving remnants of sand. I didn't shed one tear.

Lawrence was in the barn. I called out to him, "I'm done! I'm finished!" He was amazed that I was finished so quickly, and he was even more amazed that I, Melony, did not shed a tear.

Two days later, my friend Kate came into the center. "God told me to buy you something," she said hesitantly. "You will think I'm crazy."

I jokingly assured her I already thought she was, and she handed me the "gift."

I unwrapped it, inscribed on a beautiful wooden box were the words: "To the Master Carpenter's Daughter Melony ~ Jeremiah 23:29, 'Isn't my message like fire? Isn't it like a hammer shattering a rock?'"

Speechless, I opened the box. Inside was another inscription: "Melony, my beautiful, precious, and beloved daughter. 1 Peter 2:9–10, 'My chosen instrument . . . From nothing to something, from rejected to accepted.' Love your Abba Father, Daddy God!"

Nestled inside, a beautiful golden hammer glistened. It was the same as the one Peter had given me. It was a claw hammer, the same as Peter's; one side used to tear apart, and the other side used to build.

I fell apart. Whatever was left of my stony heart melted and turned into tears. "This was a gift from God," I said to Kate between sobs. "Peter wanted me to have the golden hammer, but because of his own brokenness, all he could give me was the broken one. God wanted me to have this one."

Kate said she struggled with God when she felt Him asking her to buy the hammer, saying, "Where on earth am I going to find a golden hammer?" In a store that day, was a whole stack of golden hammers.

The next week, Lawrence and I spent holiday time in the mountains. We stopped at a restaurant for lunch. Loud country music played. We asked the waitress if there was any chance she could turn it down, but the volume control was in the manager's office, which she didn't have access to. We were forced to listen, and a song played I had never heard before, called "My Daughter's Father" by Gord Bamford. The chorus said, "All I have to be is my daughter's father." I googled the lyrics, and tearily read them to Lawrence.

The chorus read:

> *It's not like everybody's waiting,*
> *To see if I'll go far,*
> *It's not like everybody's watching,*
> *Though sometimes I think they are,*
> *I don't have to change the world,*

I don't have to walk on water,
All I have to be,
Is my daughter's father.

The holiday was over. God was placing the father issue in front of me, again.

CHAPTER 38

A few days later, I gave a class presentation at a private Catholic school. It was held in the sanctuary. Half the class raised their hands when I asked if they were Christian.

I shared my story as usual but this time included the story of the hammers. I talked about the fact that the majority of the women who come into the center have father issues, that a girl's first love is her father and that if she is negatively affected by him, she will look for love elsewhere. And the same goes for a man; his first love is his mother. This will follow through to who they marry. Some will marry someone like their opposite parent to subconsciously continue trying to obtain their love.

When I used the hammers, I noticed a girl valiantly trying not to cry. Unable to contain tears any longer, in silence they washed down her cheeks. No one could see what was transpiring except me. She had not raised her hand when I asked who was a Christian.

Raising her eyes as she tried to catch her breath, she fixated on something. It was the crucifix hanging at the front of the church. I had already used the blocks, gently explaining that if they didn't receive the love they needed from their parents, it was because their parents had not removed the blocks of pain from their own lives, and therefore could not love and nurture them the way they needed.

At the end, I asked if they would allow me to pray for them. They ALL nodded their heads, and they ALL positioned themselves in prayer.

That same day at the center, I spoke with some adoptive parents. Already in his twenties, they knew their adopted son had adoption-related issues that needed to be dealt with. Unsure if their son would come in, we talked for a while but the dad wasn't saying much.

"How are you doing?" I asked him.

"I just want my son to heal," he said looking away. He tried to hold back tears.

I told him when I started working on my adoption, I had reservations because I didn't want to hurt my dad. I told him about asking Dad for his blessing to find Peter. That's when this man's tears spilled.

I asked if I could pray with them before they left. "Lord, I see two people in front of me with huge hearts, and I can see it hurts them deeply to watch their son flailing." When I finished praying, tears flowed freely from us all. Then *he* prayed. I was incredibly moved.

They were unaware that a birth mother support group was meeting in the back. And there I sat, an adoptee praying with a couple who had adopted. A voice coming up the stairs then resonated through the building. I knew the voice. It belonged to a birth father. All of us had come together in one place that night. The center was emotionally and spiritually supercharged at that moment. Only one person could've orchestrated that, God.

CHAPTER 39

In February of 2013, a major temptation arose. Lent had begun and one scripture that resonated with me was when the Spirit led Jesus into the desert to enable Satan to tempt Him. And so it started a temptation for me.

A position in the administrative field I had previously worked in opened close to home. I was told it was mine for the taking if I applied. Was Satan offering it or God? I kept telling myself it was God because I wanted it. There would be much less stress, a lucrative salary, a shorter commute, and not being as tired anymore from the emotional toll and speaking engagements. The same night I became aware of the position, I had a dream. It involved being locked in a vault where people could not hear me calling out.

I wrestled with the dream and the decision, and spoke with friends and family. They expressed concern, but were supportive of any decision, come what may. One of my go-to people for serious decisions asked where I was on a scale of one to ten on a spiritual, emotional, mental, physical, and relational level. On all levels, I said a six, except for spiritually, an eight, because at the moment I struggled to hear God.

"So your tires are forty percent deflated. Are you okay with that?" she asked.

"Yes, but tires don't last long when they are forty percent deflated."

I struggled with that statement. I told myself nothing would be left of me if I didn't leave the center. I told myself I could still minister to people after leaving. It might look different, but it would still happen.

My friend, Kate, assured me she was in major prayer and was

going to text me on Sunday to remind me that she was praying and interceding. But when she went to send the text, she felt God saying, "You may be praying, but if you send this text, you are not interceding, you are interfering."

By Sunday, ninety percent of me was sure about leaving the center. I called Dad and told him I was close to deciding. The scripture readings in church that Sunday told of God telling Abram, "Look up at the sky and count the stars, if you can. Just so, he added, shall your descendants be," Genesis 15:5, NABRE. I remembered a pastor saying, "We believe in you Melony and we want you to be a star shining brightly for a long time. We don't want you to be a comet that's here today and gone tomorrow." His words resonated as I listened to the scripture, but I told myself I would be a star shining no matter where I was.

The other scripture was, "Their God is their stomach; their glory is in their shame. *Their minds are occupied with earthly things.* But our citizenship is in heaven, and from it we also await a savior, the Lord Jesus Christ. He will change our lowly body to conform with his glorified body by the power that enables him also to bring all things into subjection to himself. Therefore, my brothers, whom I love and long for, my joy and crown, in this way *stand firm in the Lord*, beloved," Philippians 3:19–21, 4:1, NABRE. The scriptures irked me while I was trying to justify the decision I was making.

On Monday morning, I thought, "Who am I kidding?" and decided to stay at the center. By Monday afternoon, the pros outweighed the cons in favor of taking the position being offered, and the struggle started again.

Before leaving for home that day, a post-abortive client thanked me. I knew the job being offered was a thankless one. What impact would my life have five years down the road if I left or stayed? When I got home, I told Lawrence we needed to celebrate because I had made the final decision to stay at the center.

The next morning, I read in Scripture, "Whoever exalts himself will be humbled; but whoever humbles himself will be exalted," Matthew 23:12, NIV. Doubt still occupied two percent of my brain. I was still not convinced to stay.

I looked in the mirror and started to exalt myself. Patting myself on the back, I said, "You are a good person for withstanding this temptation, Melony. You are staying at the center. You should feel good about yourself." That's when the spiritual punch between the eyes came. That's when I was not so gently humbled, and a thought came to mind. It said, "Stop feeling so good about yourself, Melony. Judas gave Me up for thirty pieces of silver. Now you know what your price was." My heart broke repenting, "Oh God, forgive me."

Upon arrival at the center that morning, I told my co-worker what had happened. She had been on holiday; knowing God had removed her as the decision was being made. She knew she would've interfered but felt the need to pray while gone.

If I had left the center, I may have been physically better in five years, but spiritually, I would've been dead. Also, what God was telling me in the dream became clear. The vault represented my earlier position; in fact, there was a walk-in vault in the previous office. If I had taken the position, God would no longer have used my voice. People would no longer hear me. I had almost thrown it all away.

CHAPTER 40

In November of 2012, the first adoptee group worked through the program, and I took part with them. Part of the program involved learning how other adoptees feel and the typical behaviors used for self-protection. Learning that you're not the only one goes a long way to understanding yourself. Each chapter of the book we were studying dealt with a specific topic. We wrote letters to birth parents, never to be mailed. And we "traded shoes" and wrote letters back to ourselves *from* our birth parents with feelings and words they might have said. We read letters aloud to each other. It amazed me how much more emotion came out when something was read aloud. Each chapter ended with our written thoughts and prayers.

The following are portions of letters to my birth parents, Peter and Pearl, and letters "from" them, and some of my prayers:

December 15, 2012 – Lord, please help me on this journey to be closer to You. Help me to understand Your ways. Help me see things through Your eyes. I pray that through this I come to know You better and that I come to understand myself better. Loving myself through Your eyes will enable me to love others more freely. I pray for Your wisdom Lord. I pray for Your vision. Shelter me, Lord, when I run to You. Show me the truth Lord, so I can be free. I long to not be anxious and I long to relax in You Lord, show me how. Amen.

January 7, 2013 – Lord, I read on Christmas Day, "But to all who received Him, who believed in His name, He gave power to become children of God, who were born, not of blood or of the will of the flesh or of the will of man, but of God," John 1:12. Do You have any idea how this makes me feel? You do! It was a gift You wanted to give me, one that would seep into my psyche by the end of the year. Again I am realizing deep in my soul that I am here because You willed it! I am not a mistake! I am supposed to be here! Thank You for showing me this. I pray You continue to show me more. Give me an accepting spirit Lord. I pray You continue to clean out the corners of my heart. Amen.

January 15, 2013 – Lord, I feel even more loved by You. I know in my head You love me, but I feel it more. You love me through my anger. You expect me to be angry. Where would I be in all of this if not for You, Lord? The Message version of Ephesians 4:26 says, "Go ahead and be angry, you do well to be angry—but don't use your anger as fuel for revenge. And don't stay angry. Don't go to bed angry. Don't give the devil that kind of foothold in your life." Thank you God for showing me this! Lord, help me to use this healing for You, to build Your Kingdom. Help me to show people not to be afraid to unleash their anger. Help me to show adoptive parents that it's okay to let their children vent their anger, it's imperative! You are such a good God. Lord, You tell us that even if You were foolish, Your wisdom would be beyond any wisdom we could imagine. I ask then Lord for some of Your foolishness, and a touch of Your wisdom would be beyond anything I can imagine. Jesus, give me Your servant's heart. Let me care for those who are hurting. Amen.

January 20, 2013
Dear Pearl,

I'm supposed to be writing about my fantasies of what you are like. I know I used to think about it briefly when I was a child, (briefly because I didn't dare think about it), but not so much anymore. I, of course, now know what you looked like so that is no longer a fantasy. Thinking about it now, I do wonder what you were like as a person. That's one thing I didn't find out about. Were you kind? Were you generous? Were you loving? Were you below average intelligence like the papers from social services said you were? Were you manipulative like the papers said you were? Were you a good mom? I know you thought of me which brings me comfort. And this sounds weird, but the fact that you were in pain about the adoption also brings me comfort. It means that I meant something. What would it have been like if you would've still been alive when I found you? It's such a push-pull feeling for me. I would've liked that and yet I wouldn't have. Finding and knowing Peter unleashed a lot of anger. Would it have been the same if I had met you? There are things I will never know. And I have no idea if that's a good thing or a bad thing. It's like I'm in a state of limbo thinking about it.

January 20, 2013
Dear Melony,

You know I have fantasized about what it would've been like to keep you. I have loved you all my life. I have memories of holding you as a newborn. Oh, now I wish I had memories of you growing up. I fantasize about what your first day of school was like, what your first birthday was like, what you like to do for fun, whether or not you got married, whether or not I have grandchildren. I wonder what it would've been like to tuck you into bed at night. I wonder what it would've been like for me to tell you that I love you. I wonder what it would feel like for you to tell me that you love me. I had hoped beyond hope that you would try to find me when you turned eighteen. I had dreams of us being close, being friends. I wish you could've known me, but I don't think I could have handled any anger from you. I would've fallen apart.

January 20, 2013
Dear Peter,

I don't feel as though I really got to know you all that well. I was too busy being angry. I know that now. I think I'm lamenting the fact that I didn't take the time to know you better. But it's the same as the feelings with Pearl, even if you were still alive, there would definitely be the push-pull thing going on, subconsciously. I obviously wanted you to hurt as much as I did, so weeks would go by before I called you. You didn't "hear" my anger, but I know that by doing that, I was trying to make you "feel" it. I'm sorry

Peter. I am so sorry . . . Did I fantasize about you when I was little? No, but interestingly I divorced my husband and remarried a man eighteen years older than me. The papers said you had black hair, olive colored skin, were of German descent, and that you were Catholic. So is he. Things that make you go hmmmmmmm . . . Sometimes I don't treat my husband very well. Am I subconsciously trying to get back at you? We have come through a lot and our marriage is stronger as a result, but this has definitely opened my eyes.

———————

January 20, 2013 – Thank you Lord for all of this, I am amazed at the insights this has given me. When I looked at the title of the chapter, "I sometimes fantasize about my birth family", I didn't think it applied to me at all. Was I ever wrong! As I continue to expel all of these thoughts and emotions, I can feel myself trusting You more. I feel closer to You. You indeed DO know all of my thoughts and you have been patiently waiting for me to go THROUGH them. Thank you, God, for being by my side as I was constantly going around them. I think I have been avoiding all of this my whole life. Who am I kidding? I KNOW I have been avoiding it my whole life. I pray that You continue to open my mind, my heart, my soul, and my spirit as I go through this. Even if it is extremely painful, I trust You Lord. I know that You have a purpose. I pray that You will be glorified through all of this. I love You.

———————

February 18, 2013
Dear Peter,

It has not been easy listening to others when they talk about their family history, whether good or bad, at least they knew where they came from. I need to keep my eyes fixed on God. Ultimately He is my father, but people put so much emphasis on genealogy, (even the Bible in the Book of Matthew!), family history, and family heirlooms. I have always felt none of that was important. That's what I told myself. I told myself that because I knew I was hurting. I needed to be secure and the only way I could do that was by denying it was important. I am envious of those who know from whence they came. And now, even though I know my family tree after finding you, I'm not really a part of it anyway. Jesus knew God the father intimately and yet he felt forsaken by Him. Peter, I did not know you and yet I was forsaken by you. Should I feel privileged I was loved by you in the end? Your wife said that before you died, you told her now you knew you were leaving something behind so you were okay with dying. Should I now feel okay?

March 3, 2013
Dear Pearl,

I have always felt the need to be perfect. If that results from being adopted, then it is as it is. I have read a lot about adoption over the past few years. After finding all of this out, it's as though the "bugs are being scattered from the darkness." I understand myself more, and I realize I don't always have to be superwoman. It's taking a while and will continue to do so as I work through this, but it's happening. Part of it is a need to be perfect so that no one would ever want to "get rid of me" again. Why would they want to get rid of the perfect wife? The perfect mother? The perfect daughter? The perfect employee? The perfect friend? Oh my! Just in writing this I see my constant need to be perfect! Perhaps, there is more here than what I thought.

March 3, 2013
Dear Peter,

I think I have spent my whole life making myself subconsciously "perfect" so you would want me. A daughter is usually the apple of her father's eye. I was not that for you. Oh how I feel I have longed for that my whole life. But there was nothing I could do. You were gone. As the years slipped by, I could feel *myself trying to make myself "good" in God's eyes instead of yours. He told me He was there. You weren't. I had done so many stupid things, even giving myself away at fourteen. Whoa! I think I've had a major revelation. "I" was given away as a baby so "I" obviously meant nothing. Was I trying to regain what was lost by giving myself away? Was I trying to regain my self-worth, not realizing that by doing that, I lost even more? Do you see what happened, Peter? I meant nothing to you, so I meant nothing to myself. If I "gave myself away," then it would make "giving myself away" okay. I was trying to get you to love me. If I could get a man to love me, then subconsciously, I was getting you to love me.*

March 3, 2013 – Lord, Where would I be without you? Even though facing all of this has been incredibly hard so far, after everything that happened this week, I find myself being incredibly thankful for being adopted! You knew it all. You knew what was going to happen. You've been sitting back and waiting. Oh how I love You Lord . . . I trust You . . . Thank You that You love me just the way I am. I know that, but it is definitely gelling more and more in my heart. I cannot imagine someone going through this without You Lord. I need not compare myself with anyone. You don't love us more or less because of ANYTHING. You love me just as much as the President of the United States. You love me just as much as the Pope. You love me just as much as the homeless person on the street. You love me just as much as the leper. You love us all . . . Help me to love others and to see others the way You do, Lord.

March 11, 2013
Dear Pearl,

My fear of rejection, where do I begin? I have pushed people away from me my entire life. I have kept them at arm's length, not letting them get too close, afraid of letting them see the real me. I realize it was partly the fear of being rejected, but the other side of me wasn't letting them near because I didn't know who "I" was. I have been thinking about this whole rejection thing. I've seen people over and over try to justify something they've done, or something they're doing because of a life event. Everyone fears rejection. Is my fear more due to being rejected by you? I know the answer. It's dealing with it that's the problem. I know from your letters you were dealing with it too.

March 11, 2013
Dear Peter,

The tears fell as soon as I started writing this letter. A huge part of my rejection issues come from you. When I read you had denied paternity, you may as well have stuck a dagger in my heart. You know what I'm realizing now? There are people rejected by their fathers every day, and the father is still in their life! At least in my mind, you were dead. I had no idea who you were or how to find you, but knowing you rejected me before I was even born is incredibly painful. Oh God, it hurts. Of course I have rejection issues! Of course I've pushed people away and clung to others. I was the firstborn of you and Pearl. Yet, I did not receive any blessing from you, Peter. I got the feeling that Pearl poured her blessings out on me before she let me go. I knew that parents represent God to their children. When I read that parents are responsible for portraying God's reliability, well, how do you think that affected me? I couldn't rely on you for anything, because you denied me. You rejected me. You shunned me. My dad stepped up and took your place, Peter. But even then, I didn't feel totally protected. I feel the last wisps of anger dissipating. I am so grateful for paper and pen.

March 11, 2013 – Oh Lord, where would I be without You? How many times have I said that? You knew exactly what Peter and

Pearl would do. You wanted me to go through this. You knew exactly how I would feel. You were waiting for me to return to You. You were waiting for me to hand this pain over to You. You have been waiting a long time. It has been slowly wafting its way up to You; a sacrificial aroma. Thank You for bringing me through this thus far. I pray, Lord, that You will continue to light the way. I know You will. This heart stuff hurts so bad, Lord. No wonder no one wants to go through it. You kept telling me You didn't want my burnt offerings and sacrifices. How could I love with my whole heart if I'm not willing to hand all of its hurts over to you? You made it. You know best how to love it. You know best how to care for it. Help me, Lord. Help me to continue to go to the deepest parts of my heart. Take away my fear, Lord. Replace it with Your perfect love. Amen.

March 25, 2013
Dear Pearl,

I find it interesting that they try to soften everything by using the words "relinquishment" or "placed." Everyone tries to smooth it over, to make it less than what it is. Yesterday, I took some clothing to the church. The kids were having a clothing drive. There was nothing wrong with it; in fact, more of it was good quality dress clothes that I just don't wear anymore. I didn't "relinquish" the clothes. I gave them away. It has always bothered me when people try to pussyfoot around things. Just tell it like it is and then let me deal with it! So the question really is: Do I have low self-esteem because you gave me away? The answer is yes, yes I did. If I dared to try something, I always had to try exceptionally hard because I wanted to ensure that I was good. I had to feel worthy. It created my worth by being good at something. If I didn't think that I had a chance of being good at it, I didn't dare try it. That would mean I had failed. And I already felt bad enough about myself as it was. My worth was not in who

I was. It was in what I did. If I looked at my worth in terms of who I was, well, I couldn't do that. I was given away, like a piece of clothing that didn't fit anymore or didn't look good anymore. Over the past few years, I have started to see "who I am in Christ," thank You God. I couldn't look at "who I was" in you, Pearl, because I obviously wasn't worth enough to keep. I wasn't worth the anguish that you would've gone through. I know that you went through tremendous anguish in giving me away, Pearl. But these are the feelings that I have as a result of you doing that. These feelings had permeated through me. I'm just telling you the way it was. It's the truth. And I have to wade through all of this; otherwise I will never truly know my value in Christ. As I go through all of this, things are starting to become much clearer. I don't want to hurt you, Pearl. I am grateful that this is between me and God. These have been my feelings. It is as it is.

———————

March 25, 2013
Dear Melony,

You're right. I know that you need to wade through all of this. Your feelings need to be validated. And no one should ever say that you shouldn't be feeling them. It would be like saying you aren't worthy of having them. I know that I needed to work through all of the feelings of giving you away, my entire life. And I was unable to wade through them. I was unable to work through them. These feelings were birthed in you the day that I gave you away. And you have been going through intense labor pains, your heart groaning as you separate yourself from these toxic emotions and deliver them to God.

———————

March 25, 2013
Dear Peter,

You know from what I wrote Pearl that I have always had self-esteem problems. I would basically ditto the same letter to you.

March 25, 2013
Dear Melony,

I know where your feelings stem from. I let Pearl down. I let you down. I was not what I was supposed to be. And because of that, you have not totally let God be what He is supposed to be to you. Let Him protect you. Let Him shelter you. Let Him provide for you. Let Him feed you. Let Him clothe you. And most of all, for His Son's sake, let Him love you, Melony . . . Let Him be all the things that I was not . . . I love you.

April 7, 2013
Dear Pearl,

God has wanted me to work through this. Am I ready to thank you for the part you played in the making of my personality? I think I am. I am thankful for you, Pearl. I am thankful God used you as the vessel—as His handmaiden. I know you prayed. That was clear from your letters. If you prayed, then you were His Handmaiden, Pearl. Mary knew that what lay ahead of her would be extremely hard. But she trusted God. I believe that's what happened with you also, Pearl. You didn't view yourself as a handmaiden of His, but you were. You are. And I believe you are in heaven serving Him right now.

April 7, 2013
Dear Melony,

You know that I chastised myself my whole life because of this event. Now that I'm in heaven, I see the bigger picture. Thank you for viewing me in this new light Melony, my precious daughter. Thank you for viewing me in His light . . .

April 7, 2013
Dear Peter,

As weird as this sounds, I do thank you. I knew that God was using all of this to mould and shape me. And I know that

*He loves me for me. How do I say in a loving way that I thank
you for everything you've done, Peter? I wish that you could hear
my words, see the look on my face, hear the tone of my voice . . .
There is no anger, no malice. I know that I would not be who I
am if not for you, Peter. I have stopped "beating you up". Please
stop beating yourself up, if you are. God loves you. And so do I.*

---

*April 7, 2013 – Lord, you have shown me before what my life's
purpose is. I ask that if there is more You want me to do, open
the doors further, Lord. Open the doors that need to be opened,
and close the doors that need to be closed. If there are spiritual
gifts I haven't been using because of not wanting to walk through
this pain, I ask for Your forgiveness for avoiding it all this time.
But I believe "there is a time for everything—a season for everything." Second, I ask You to show me the spiritual gifts I haven't
been using. Open my eyes, Lord. Open the gates of my mind, my
heart, my spirit, and my soul.*

April 18, 2013
Dear Pearl,

*What a rollercoaster ride this has been! Emotions have been
all over the place for months. I thank you, Pearl for not taking
what would've looked like the easier choice of aborting me. It's
interesting now as I look back at myself, I know I dishonoured
you by having my abortion. I am grateful to you, Pearl. Were you
being led by God to place me for adoption? I don't know, but I
do know I would not be who I am if you hadn't. Yes, it radically
changed both of our lives, but we would've both had pain either
way. I had another adoptee ask me the other day if I felt driven.
He said that someone told him adoptees typically feel driven.
I know I was that way before, because I was trying to prove my
worth to you, Pearl, but now I am driven by the Holy Spirit.
The drive to prove my worth got me to where I was in my life. In
society's eyes, I had done well for myself. That drive was part of*

my personality. Now I have given God the reigns to my passion and drive. It is being used to glorify Him. Thank you, Pearl. I love you.

May 19, 2013 – Oh Lord . . . How can I thank You for bringing me through this? When I think of the amount of pain that I have caused by "rejecting before I was rejected," I almost want to vomit. I saw myself as a source of pain to others—as though it was my purpose in life. I have caused so much pain Lord . . . some pain that others don't even know about. How do I make up for that? Oh Lord, how much You must love me. How many times has Satan tried to bring me down various times through rejection, but You have totally turned it around. You planted Your banner in me the day I was born, actually before I was conceived. I was rejected by Peter before I was even born. You knew what was going to happen. My heritage is not where I came from. My identity is not caught up in worldly things. My heritage and identity is in YOU! Yes, it has been a battle Lord. Thank you for protecting me on all sides with your warring angels. I pray for Your continued anointing Lord. I praise You Lord . . . I love You Lord . . . I worship You Lord . . .

May 20, 2013
Dear Pearl,

To say I have changed as a result of going through all of this would be the understatement of the year, the understatement of my life! I continue to realize so many things. God has brought me through this kicking and screaming, waiting with the patience only He could have as I went through my temper tantrums. I knew it would not be easy, but I had to be obedient, no matter how painful. He had told me He would "meet me on the other side." It was not a calm sea He had asked me to cross, it was a stormy one. And He met me right smack dab in the middle of it. I don't know how many times I got out of the boat and walked

toward Him, only to sink in my pain. But He never let go Pearl.
He was lovingly and patiently throwing another life line for me
to grab and hold onto as He dragged me back into the boat, into
the safety of His arms. I can't help feeling as though a part of you
died when this happened to you. If it is possible, I pray this gives
you inexplicable joy. I pray it resurrects that part of your life
Pearl. I am very close to coming to terms with who I am. I feel
complete. I feel whole. You have been standing there with Jesus,
cheering me on. Thank you, Pearl.

May 27, 2013
Dear Peter,

I have come so far Peter. I can't tell you how it fully feels or
explain clearly enough how much I have come through and
where I am now. But I do see how God wants people to face and
move through their pain, how He is beckoning to them. And I see
how badly Satan wants them to stay where they're at. If we move
through our pain, we can help others. And if we move through
it, we will help others a hundred times more effectively. Yes, God
uses broken, unhealed people to help others, but how much more
He can use us when we are healed! I can still use the hammer
you gave me Peter, even though it's broken. But how much
stronger could I hit something if I'm not worried the hammer
will fly apart? I am almost through this Peter. I am almost fully
restored and I am preparing myself for how much more God will
use me. I am no longer broken. Psalm 31:13 says, "I am forgotten,
out of mind like the dead; I am like a shattered dish." I was
shattered Peter. But God has been patient. He has glued all the
pieces back together and we are together now just waiting for
everything to dry.

It has been incredibly gratifying watching adoptees, young
and old, learn "who they are" as they progress through the
program. Sometimes it's hard to know where you're going in

life or how you can lead others, if you don't know where you came from.

LIFE LESSON #32: *"If Moses' cultural and family history had been expunged by his adoption into Pharaoh's household, how would he have known who he was to fulfill God's call to lead the Israelites out of slavery."—Rick Uhrlaub*

The next letter was prophetic, considering what happened two days later on June 1, 2013.

May 30, 2013 – Father, Son, and Holy Spirit, I choose You, Lord. I choose comfort in the safety of Your arms. I choose to not be anxious about Your love, Lord. I've been running my whole life. And I've been trying to wear other people's armor throughout the battles in my life. You have been standing there with the right one this whole time, waiting for me to fall from sheer exhaustion so that You could put it on me. I choose to have the most intimate relationship and friendship with You, Lord. I went for a walk on Sunday. I have been feeling as though You have been preparing me for future battles. As I was walking, I started noticing various rocks. I picked up different ones, remembering the five smooth stones David picked up to slay Goliath. After throwing some back and picking up better ones, I ended up with five in my pocket. When I got home, it was as though I had an instant download from You. You told me I had walked through my adoptee pain so I would fully understand who I am, but especially who I am in You. And I needed to know this so I will be comfortable wearing the armor You have given me for the future battles that lie ahead. The stones are on my desk at home. Thank You, Lord. I love You.

PART VI

Death and Life

CHAPTER 41

God asked His disciple, Peter three times if he loved Him. His question to me has always been, "Do you trust me?" I lost count of the number of times He has asked me that question.

On June 1st, 2013, our world turned upside down. My daughters, Jodie and Lindsey, my two youngest grandsons, seven-year-old Alex and two-year-old Ronan, and I, drove to Alberta to stay with my sister and visit family. I had chosen that weekend to go. It was one of the few weekends that worked for all of our schedules. My oldest grandson, nine-year-old Austin, stayed behind with his dad, my son-in-law, Aaron.

We shot off fireworks and were sitting around a bonfire. Earlier in the evening we noticed an upside-down rainbow straight above us, a weird phenomenon. I wondered what kind of twist this was of one of God's promises.

We sat around the fire, laughing and grateful for the time we could spend together. That's when the call came. Jodie's face went ashen. She handed me the phone and took off, running across the yard. Everyone ran after her. It was Lindsey's husband, my other son-in-law, on the phone.

"Aaron has been in a motorcycle accident," he said chokingly. "They're loading him up in an EMS now."

My mind raced. "What are you saying? Is he going to be okay?"

"No," he said as his voice was caught in his throat. "He's gone."

"What are you saying?" I screamed in the phone. "Are you telling me he's dead?"

Then came that word. "Yes."

Everything changed.

Alex stood there, looking lost and confused. Chaos reigned. Everyone else was inside the house. I grabbed him and sat by the fire for a few minutes, rocking him, tears flowing.

It was as though the evil one was sitting there with a big grin, saying, "Where's your God now?"

"Grandma, what's wrong?" he asked feebly, not wanting to know the answer. That's when I did the one thing no grandmother should ever have to do. I told him his dad had died.

My family tried to figure out how to get us back quickly while the rest of us watched the dark door of mourning being opened to invite us in. We loaded up into two vehicles, making the ten-hour trip back home in eight hours, in the middle of the night so we could make it back by early morning. Jodie still needed to tell Austin. He was sleeping overnight at a friend's house, oblivious to what had happened.

I sat in the front seat of one vehicle as my brother-in-law drove. Jodie, Alex, and Ronan were in the back. No one slept. Two-year-old Ronan's eyes glassed over as he looked into the black-hole opening to him beyond the door of mourning. He held onto Jodie's hand from his car seat, seemingly aware that she was the only parent he had left.

We stopped a few times, Alex's body desperate to vomit out this spiritual pain that invaded his soul. I reached back and touched Jodie's leg. She gazed out the window at her future, tears streaming down her face. The sun was rising.

Oh Jodie, I thought, listening to the drone of tires. *If I could make the sun go back a day, I would.*

When she was a baby and she cried, I picked her up and comforted her and everything was all right. As she grew up, when she fell and skinned her knees, I picked her up, kissing it better as I applied a Band-Aid; softly telling her everything would be all right. But there was nothing I could do to make this all right. No number of Band-Aids would ever cover this wound. No amount of comforting would make this okay. As a mother, I was helpless, but I sensed God asking me, "Melony, do you trust that I will take care of your daughter and your grandsons?"

I called the family's home where Austin was staying to alert them that someone would be there to pick him up. It was very early. His friend's dad groggily answered the phone. They had not yet heard what had happened. I told him to not tell Austin. This would allow Jodie to tell him in his own home, although we knew nothing would soften this blow.

After Jodie told him, I walked into the room. And there it was, the look in his eyes that only death can bring. The endless stream of people came, one of them being Austin's friend's dad, the one who answered the phone that morning. "I didn't want to let Austin leave our house," he said, his voice filling with despair. "I didn't want to let him go because I knew what he would face when he got home."

We all slept fitfully that night. The boys slept with Jodie and I slept in Austin's room. At five in the morning, Aaron's alarm went off, a reminder of what once was but would never be again. I could hear Jodie get up and go to what had been his side of the bed to shut it off, and so, started life without him.

His funeral was held in the arena a few days later. My family traveled out to grieve with us. My dad was in the guest room of our home the morning of Aaron's funeral. "Dad? Are you awake?" I whispered as I poked my head around the door.

"Yes", he whispered.

I sat on his bed. At eighty-nine years of age, his body was weakening more and more, but there was nothing that would keep him from being there for Jodie, his oldest granddaughter.

I remembered listening to a particular Bible study on the book of Esther. The teacher of the study talked about the "pivot point of peripety" in Esther's life. A peripety is a *sudden and unexpected change of fortune or reverse of circumstances.* The pivot point can be a seemingly unimportant moment, but it is the catalyst of the peripety.

As I looked at dad, I remembered almost giving Jodie away when she was born, my heart almost being broken, "like a shattered dish," the psalmist lamented. But as I pondered giving Jodie away, dad had come into my bedroom to find me crying. As he sat on my bed and stroked my hair, he didn't tell me that I had made my bed and now I had to lie in it. He didn't tell me to straighten up and pull myself together. He told me that if this was the way this would affect me, I'd better keep her.

That was the pivot point of peripety—the moment that altered the destiny of Jodie's life and mine, a moment that would alter generations.

That morning in my guest room, the day we would bury Jodie's husband, my grandson's father, I asked Dad if he would bless the boys. I had no idea whether Aaron had ever blessed his sons. With tears already streaming down Dad's face, he said he would be honored.

What were the boys doing at that exact moment as Dad held my hands and prayed for them and blessed them? Were they still asleep? Were they staring anxiously off into space? Were they playing? Could they feel the spiritual blessing coming from the mouth of this man who had loved me unconditionally my whole life? As a butterfly fluttered around the arena the day of Aaron's funeral, a thousand onlookers and the boys were oblivious of Dad's words of blessing that morning.

Weeks later, I struggled through my first day back at the center. It was Baby Bottle Campaign time, one of the major fundraisers for the center. Bottles were being dropped off, with volunteers busy counting the cheques, cash, and change in them. My assistant came into my office with a cheque in her hand. "I thought you might like to see this," she said.

I looked at it. We were always thankful for all the funds we received, but this one was unusual. It was a cheque from a doctor, for a higher than normal amount. A memory flooded my brain. My throat constricted. I tried to stop the tears, but it was useless.

I knew the doctor who wrote the cheque. Jodie had called me a few months earlier saying, "Hey Mom, there's a praise and worship service at a church in town tonight. Do you want to go to it with me?" I jumped at the chance of worshiping with her.

When we arrived, it was just as it should be—people of every denomination, praising and worshiping God. We could hear them singing as we approached the door.

But the night was not just about praising and worshiping. It was about praying for someone. The specific someone was *this* doctor. He was a loving husband and father. And he had cancer. It was not survivor friendly.

As he spoke of his struggle, he talked of one night in particular. He had cried all night, asking God why this was happening. He talked about wrestling with God and succumbing, finally, to acceptance, and trust. Then he said words that now poured back into my mind. "Tonight is not about me. It's about praising and worshiping Jesus Christ. I've become thankful for this cancer. I am thankful for it because it has brought me closer to Him than I have ever felt."

The words came back to life as I held his cheque in my hand. I saw men all the time at the center who did not want to be fathers. I wrestled with God, asking Him why he would take my son-in-law, who loved his sons and loved being a dad. But God did not answer the question. He just kept asking me if I trusted Him.

Did I feel closer to God? Yes. Was I thankful for the circumstances? No. I could feel God asking me again, "Do you trust Me Melony?"

"Yes," I answered. "Yes I do."

I prayed that one day Aaron's death would draw my grand-sons closer to Him.

CHAPTER 42

I advised my family to be mindful and careful of any decisions being made. When grieving, our brains do not run at full capacity. I thought I was exempt.

One night I forgot my phone at the center. I had become like so many people; my life's schedule, contacts, everything was on my phone. And then I arrived at home to find the internet not working.

I had a morning schedule that included sipping coffee while checking the weather forecast, looking at the daily scripture readings, and then checking my email—all via the internet, then praying. Without internet, my morning schedule was rudely interrupted. I couldn't check the weather or look up the scrip-ture readings on the phone because I had forgotten it. My mind was so dysfunctional that it did not even occur to me to turn the radio on to hear the weather forecast or to pick up my Bible to read scripture.

Lawrence was still sleeping. I sat there for a minute, dis-traught until God spoke to my heart saying, "Excuse me but I AM the one in control here. I caused you to forget your phone, and I shut down your internet so you could take a moment and just sit with Me. Let Me remind you how much I love your fam-ily and you, and that I will help them get through this. Please take time this morning and just be still and know I am God."

I got the message, loud and clear.

Four and a half months later, I stood in a dressing room, looking at an outfit I contemplated buying for the center's fundraising banquet scheduled that week. My cell phone rang, the next life changing call.

It was my sister. "Dad has had a stroke," she said, taking in sharp breaths. "He's been airlifted to Calgary."

I drove home fast, stopping at Lindsey and Rod's home. My phone rang again, this time my brother. "They're still running tests. Mel, they give him two hours to two days to live. He's unable to talk, but we can tell that he understands what we're saying."

I asked if I could talk to Dad, knowing it might be the last words I would ever say to him. My brother assured me they would call as soon as Dad was back in his room.

The phone rang as I drove in the yard. My sister held the phone up to Dad's ear. I stood outside the garage, sobbing into the phone, "I love you so much, Dad! If you need to go before I get there, don't wait for me."

Why was God taking him now? Dad was my rock, the one I "grieved out" to. I flew out the next morning, having no idea if he would be gone by the time I arrived.

A few months earlier, if it was possible to make time stand still so that my family could avoid pain, I would have. Now, if I could have time fast forward so I could be with my dad, I would have, but somehow I made it.

Within a few minutes after I entered his hospital room, I took out the same anointing oil I had used to anoint Peter, and

I anointed my dad. It was one of the most painful, yet one of the most holy times I had ever encountered.

Even though his brain was eighty-five percent hemorrhaged, he knew who we all were for the first couple of days. He couldn't speak, yet he smiled when we joked with him, and tears slid down his cheeks when we cried.

Dad always believed everything happens for a reason. He was not in the palliative ward, because there wasn't any room. He was in the cardiac ward. It was a learning experience for most of the nurses. Most had not yet experienced someone dying. Two of them told us later, they were now thinking of becoming palliative nurses.

The first night, my sister and I slept together on the same gurney in Dad's room. We all slept fitfully. I laid there and listened to Dad breathing, in, out, in, out, in, out. He had what was termed a "death rattle," a horrible gurgling sound every time he took a breath. One nurse told us they would all stand at the nurse's station and talk about Dad. They couldn't get over how we all camped out in his room, not leaving his side.

The doctor came in on the third morning to find us all still camped. "Wow," he whispered, "your dad must've done something right in his life to have this much support."

Yes. He did. He loved us all unconditionally our whole lives.

His death was perfect. The last couple of days he was drugged heavily to help with the pain and heavy, laboured breathing. The day before he died, as we wrote his obituary, I looked up to see a perfect cross made by jet trails in the sky. It was surreal.

By the fourth day, we smelled ripe after being in the same clothes for four days. My sister and I took turns having a bath in Dad's hospital bathroom. I was standing there, drying my hair afterward. "This is just too weird," I said. "Here I am blow-drying my hair and my dad is laying here on his deathbed."

My brother said, "If a baby had just been born in this room, would you be doing the same thing? Everyone has a b-day and everyone has a d-day."

"Yes!" I exclaimed. Everything was put into perspective with that statement. Dad would've loved what we were doing.

My sister and I shaved Dad's face, sensing this would be the day. I had given him a scripture ring two years prior. It was in my pocket. About an hour before he died, I read him four different psalms, the last being Psalm 23.

After four days of struggling, he took his last breath. We sat with him for a while and I anointed him again, afterward moving my hands just above his skin as I prayed.

I reached into my pocket, pulled the ring out, and placed it on his pinkie. It was the biggest size I could get but Dad's hands were so big that he could only wear it on his pinkie. His heart was as big as his hands.

I remembered how upset he was when he had been out to visit and lost the ring. A few days later, I found it. I couldn't remember the scripture engraved on the ring. Staring in disbelief, it was Psalm 23.

I sat in the back seat of the vehicle as my brother-in-law drove that night. At 3:00 in the morning as we drove, a song came on the radio. It was one of Dad's favorites, "What a Wonderful World" by Louis Armstrong.

I see trees of green, red roses too,
I see them bloom for me and you.
And I think to myself what a wonderful world.

I see skies of blue and clouds of white,
The bright blessed the day, the dark sacred night.
And I think to myself what a wonderful world.

The colors of the rainbow so pretty in the sky,
Are also on the faces of people going by.

I see friends shaking hands saying how do you do,
But what they're really saying is I love you.

I hear baby's crying, and I watched them grow,
They'll learn much more than I'll ever know.
And I think to myself what a wonderful world.
Yes, I think to myself what a wonderful world.

I smiled through my tears as I listened to the song. One thing I whispered to Dad before he died was that he was a spiritual grandfather to hundreds of babies.

On the flight back, a young man sat beside me in the terminal. When we got on the plane, his seat was beside mine. "Apparently, we are supposed to meet," I said as I smiled.

A young woman sat to my left. I told them the events of the last few days. The young man was the father of two little girls. I explained why his role as a father was so important.

The young woman said, "I ditto everything she said. I'm a daddy's girl and my dad has had a huge impact on my life."

"I think I need to start spending more time at home," he whispered.

Upon hearing Dad had died, my seven-year-old grandson, Alex, said, "Well now both Grandma and us no longer have a dad." Again, God's timing was perfect. My grandsons now believed they could relate to me even more.

Dad wasn't perfect. But he was the best earthly father example of my Heavenly Father. Just like God, he loved us unconditionally. Just like God, he disciplined us. He wasn't perfect, but he was now with The Perfect One.

CHAPTER 43

A few months later, my brothers and sister and I decided on a tombstone to commemorate Dad. He requested his ashes be spread at the base of a beautiful waterfall close to where he had lived. We honored the request, but kept a small amount of ashes. They were to be buried at the base of a tombstone in the cemetery near the family farm where he grew up. Dad was gone. Nothing and no one could replace him. But this grave was the physical representation that he had been here, that he had existed.

My sister flew in from Calgary for the weekend. The plan was to drive to the cemetery to pick a spot for the tombstone. In the meantime, Jodie was scheduled for surgery the same day for a female issue, (NOT an abortion). I didn't think it a problem. The hospital staff indicated Jodie was to be ready for pick up later in the afternoon. We could easily drive the hour and a half to the cemetery, pick a spot, and be back in time.

After being admitted, we were directed to the women's health clinic. "Oh God," I said, "That's where the abortions are performed."

I stayed in the waiting room until she was called in, then my sister and I started the drive out to the cemetery. Halfway there, the hospital called. Jodie was finished. We turned around. Not a problem, we would take her with us to the cemetery. She could sleep off the anesthetic in the back seat.

As I was escorted further into the clinic, I heard the sound of metal on metal as a nurse pulled back the paper-thin sheets acting as a wall between each patient, asking each woman if they were okay.

I wanted to scream out, "Of course they aren't okay!" Here we were, right in the middle of Satan's playground with my daughter having surgery in *this* place. Jodie came staggering out, white as a ghost, still very much under the influence of the sedation, being steadied by a nurse.

We got her to the car, and she fell asleep instantly. Later in the day, Jodie experienced pain in her shoulder so intense breathing became difficult. The physician at emergency diagnosed something we had never heard of before, *referred pain*—pain that can occur elsewhere in the body, nowhere near the actual place of surgery or injury.

We stayed with her for two days. At times, the pain was so unbearable, that she could not get up on her own. By the end of the weekend, everyone was exhausted, but God used the whole incident to teach a valuable lesson.

This is true for emotional pain as well. A person can be in extreme emotional pain, but it may not show up the way you would think. A definition of referred pain is "pain from deep structures perceived as arising from a surface area remote from its actual origin." So reactions to emotional triggers can seem like they stem from something else or come out of the blue, but they are really symptoms of a deeper problem.

LIFE LESSON #34: Many people have deep rooted issues. Unfortunately, everyone, including themselves, wants to treat the "surface" issue and are afraid to tackle the root.

CHAPTER 44

The first Christmas without Aaron would not be an easy one. It was the year of "firsts" for Jodie and the boys without him. Our Christmas Eve tradition requires everyone to come together to eat heartily with much laughing and joking, followed by singing Christmas carols and opening gifts.

Hearts heavy, we fumbled through the motions. Just before Christmas, the boys stayed overnight. I had done a lot of reading on how children grieve.

Ronan, now three, continued to "act out" Aaron's death. "Grandma, this is how Daddy died, just like this," he said, lying on the floor with his eyes closed, pretending to be dead. My heart was in my mouth each time, knowing not to tell him to stop. It was his way of processing what happened. It was his way of "letting it out."

Alex, soon to be eight, continued to ask questions about who would take care of them if Mommy died and whether there would be enough money for food.

Austin, turning ten, showed signs of anger. He was a goalie on the local hockey team. Aaron had been an assistant coach on the team and spent hours and hours with him at the rink. Austin faced constant reminders he no longer had a dad; even simple things like the fact that Aaron wasn't there to tie up his skates.

The night they stayed overnight, the anger was erupting again. After tormenting his brothers, Austin ran to the spare room, hiding in the closet. I could hear him crying and whimpering. I sat beside the closet door, Ronan followed behind. Alex, wise beyond his years, came in and escorted Ronan out of the room saying, "Ronan, this is not our business."

My heart broke, listening as Austin cried. "Grandma, I don't want to be on the earth anymore," he whimpered. It was one of the hardest things my heart heard.

"Austin, it's clear you're angry Dad is gone. Hurting people hurt people and I've watched you trying to hurt your brothers. It will take a while to release the anger, but I have an idea."

A large package of paper towels sat in the closet. I asked him to come to the living room. I held the package saying, "Okay, kick and punch this package with everything you've got." He looked at me warily, unsure what to do.

"Go ahead!" I said gritting my teeth in determination. "Go for it!"

He started hitting and punching the package. Alex joined in. The package exploded with individual packages of paper towel flying across the room. I grabbed two and held them up again.

They both kept kicking and punching the packages until their emotions were spent. This was the start of many more conversations about emotions.

LIFE LESSON #35: At the root of most anger is hurt. If it's not eliminated, it takes on a life of its own. Ephesians 4:26 (MSG) says: "Be angry, you do well to be angry." God knows emotions need to be let out in a healthy way, but He does not want someone else to get hurt as we release our anger.

CHAPTER 45

In the spring, God placed an idea in my head to have a "seminar" where all the sides of the adoption triad could come together to discuss its ramifications. I was frustrated with the common Christian perception that adoption "fixes everything" and gives everyone the "warm fuzzies" and causes no pain.

One church in particular, the same one where I started my adoption healing, had a heart for adoption. I recalled hearing a woman speak. She was from outside of the country, and God had called her to adopt children with special needs. It was not uncommon for her to see people, who had not grieved infertility, adopt a child to try to fill the void. She had said to her audience, "If you are planning to adopt, and are doing it to fulfill a need in yourself, get a dog." I wanted to jump up and applaud!

A woman had called the center once, wanting to adopt. Explaining we were not an adoption agency and could not give the name of potential adoptive parents to clients placing for adoption, we talked further. She experienced an abortion years earlier and now could not conceive.

I asked her if she had emotionally and spiritually healed from the abortion. "Oh no, I don't need to do that," she replied curtly.

The more she talked, the clearer it became she was subconsciously trying to replace the aborted child. A common thread throughout our conversation was her need to make up to God for the abortion. But nothing would replace the child. She had not yet learned that nothing can "make up" for what we've done. God first wants our hearts; not our sacrifices.

Later, news came that she adopted a child. I prayed—for her and the child.

The seminar we put on was the first for any church in the city. There were sixty participants. Birth mothers, birth fathers, people pondering placing for adoption, adoptive parents, potential adoptive parents, and adoptees came together. There was more used Kleenex on the floor than I had seen in a long time.

Birth mothers spoke of pain, adoptive parents talked of the joys and struggles of adopting, and adoptees shared joys and pain. I spoke about how children grieve and how adoptive parents need to "be with" their adopted child and allow them to show their emotions. I used Ronan as an example, saying, "He has lost his father. Should we not allow him to grieve? Placing a baby in the arms of adoptive parents is like telling the baby their mother and father is gone; but it's okay, here's a new one."

One of the most hurtful things said to someone who miscarried a child is, "Well, you will have other children." Or to someone who has lost a child, "Well, thank goodness you have other children."

People are not replaceable. Parents are not replaceable. Children are not replaceable. They are all individuals whose loss needs to be grieved. There's a far deeper root at the heart of unplanned pregnancy than people recognize.

CHAPTER 46

Again, I noticed people scrambling to treat surface, "referred pain," never taking time to find the source of its deep root. Every time a woman came into the center, whether an abortion-minded client or someone post-abortive, I asked what kind of relationship they had with their father.

The answer was typically the same. The relationship was either not good or it did not exist. That was when the butterfly came to mean far more than I could ever imagine. . . .

One particular woman had fiercely held onto the pain of her abortion for forty years. It was hers. She knew it well. It twisted and warped her God-given traits. When she looked in the mirror, she did not see the person God intended. Climbing the ladder of life, she was unsure what her ladder leaned on for support.

But God had planted a seed of hope in her four years earlier, after hearing me speak at a church. God spoke to someone that day. I felt it in my bones. But not a soul approached afterward, and the seed lay dormant. God was in relentless pursuit of this woman, waiting patiently, watching her trying valiantly to stay in control of the pain, watching her trying desperately to manage it.

To others, everything appeared to be okay on the surface. There were no signs of struggle, no signs of drowning. But drowning victims are seldom seen thrashing. No one can see the struggle beneath the surface. She was losing the battle and was sinking.

With trepidation, she reached out to the lifeline God had thrown to her four years earlier, and made the call to the center. The season for healing began.

She was unable to recall the last time she cried. She learned at an early age how to sweep things under the carpet, and her carpet was dirty. She realized if she kept pretending the dirt wasn't there, it would never be clean.

I asked her to describe in writing what the emotional wound from her abortion looked like. Here is what she wrote:

Years after my abortion, I felt that if anyone became a part of my life, I would somehow disappoint them or hurt them. Now even more years later, I feel stuck in every area of my life. It seems like I can no longer do the simplest tasks. Everything seems to be an effort. I feel like I repel people. I am toxic, and I'm full of rage.

The wound began healing. Exasperated at the slow pace at times, she pressed on, starting to see glimpses in the mirror of the woman she knew from so long ago. Looking straight into the face of the shame and anger that controlled her for so many years, a light shone in the dark corners of her soul, and the ugliness scattered. She decided it was time to plan the memorial for her child. It was time to give her child honor and dignity.

I asked her to think of something meaningful she could do at the service. She prayed and pondered for two weeks. "I want to get a chrysalis." I had never heard of the word.

"Oh!" she exclaimed, "it's a cocoon. I found one when I was young, I put it in a jar and kept it on the mantle. One day, I saw movement in the cocoon. Slowly, painfully, a butterfly emerged, struggling so hard I thought it needed help. With a pair of scissors, I cut open the cocoon."

"Wow! What happened?"

"The butterfly had a big body and droopy wings. It crawled around inside the jar. After a few days, I thought its wings might spread out. But it died. Then I found out a butterfly looks the same way when coming out of its cocoon; with a big body and droopy wings. But it's the struggle that makes the butterfly strong. It then pushes the fluid from its body into its wings. So, I want to get a chrysalis and God willing, the butterfly will emerge on the day of the memorial for my aborted child. I am a new creation in Christ. And God has given me the strength to face this pain. The struggle to face this has made me strong enough to stand on my feet again. Now I'm strong enough to fly." The picture of this emerging butterfly sent tears down my face.

Another woman came into my office around the same time. Knowing there was pain that needed to be dealt with, she had previously picked up the phone numerous times, only to hang up.

One day she came to the center, wanting to volunteer. She had told God if I was available that day, it would be a sign she was to talk with me. I was available, so she knocked on my office door.

I already knew this woman and recognized her. "Hi! How are you doing? Come on in!" I exclaimed. I assumed she just wanted to say hi, but her eyes said otherwise. She looked like a deer in the headlights, ready to bolt at any second.

"C-can I talk with you for a moment?" she stammered. "Oh this is silly. I shouldn't be wasting any of your time." She started to walk away.

"You aren't wasting my time. Please come in and sit down."

"There's something that needs to be dealt with," she said. "It's affecting everything, but I don't think my pain is big enough. I haven't had an abortion or anything like that. I'm struggling with my trust in God. I'm not sure if He's there for me, and I don't know why." She cried out, "No one really knows me."

After a few minutes of sharing, the source of pain showed itself. "I might have an idea of what the problem is. Many times, when someone can't trust God, there is a very deep root. There is a subconscious connection in our heads between our earthly father and our spiritual father. And if there have been problems with our earthly father—" She stopped me before I finished.

"Oh, I have no issues with my father," she said. "He was never there for me."

I said nothing. I didn't have to. God was asking her to honor her father, and we both knew it would be difficult to follow this commandment, which was the only one with a promise attached.

At the time, I had already been thinking about starting a program to help people with father pain. Again, every time I asked someone if they thought God would provide and they answered no, I asked if their earthly father had provided for them. The answer was no. Every time I asked if they thought God would protect them, and they answered no, I asked if their earthly father had protected them. The answer was no. Every time I asked someone if God would be there for them, and they answered no, I asked if their earthly father had been there for them. The answer was no.

Would she be willing to be the first person in the "Where were you, Daddy?" program? She decided to do it, and it was intense. To describe her emotional wound, she wrote, *I'm standing on the edge of an abyss. It is dark, deep, and ugly. I'm scared to move any closer as I may fall in and be lost forever.*

She searched her heart for forgiveness, knowing in her head

that "hurting people hurt people." She was sure she had forgiven her father for everything.

"Okay, I will ask the litmus test question. Are you ready?" I said. She nodded.

"You have said your father became a Christian before he died."

"Yes, yes he did," she responded.

"Then tell me how you might feel when you see him in heaven."

Once again, she looked like a deer in the headlights. Her eyes cast down, she said, "I'm sorry. I can't."

She had memories of her father, but the ones that lingered, were not good ones. Sharing a memory, she began to realize the impact on her life. The pain started to move and slowly, ever so slowly, it started to break free from its foundation. It rocked her to a depth she had not known was there.

"This is so hard," she said, choking through sobs.

"Yes, it is, but you will be stronger by going through this. There's a story about a butterfly you need to hear." I told her about the chrysalis idea a post-abortive mother had planned for her aborted child's memorial.

As the post-abortive woman prepared for the memorial, she encountered setbacks. "I'm not sure if I can do the memorial right now," she cried as we talked on the phone that day.

"You are strong. You can do this." I asked God to give the right words to say as I prayed and struggled to encourage her. At that precise moment, a gentle chime sounded on the computer. An email had arrived. It was from the woman walking through her father pain. The subject line was "butterfly story."

Her email said, "You have no idea the impact you had on me when you told me that butterfly story. Someone else had a similar experience and put the story on the internet."

"You will not believe who just sent me an email," I said excitedly. "I have a lady in the father pain program, who was struggling the other day. I told her your butterfly story. She just sent an email with another butterfly story found online. Just when you need encouragement in your struggle, she sends the story. The story has come back to encourage you."

"Th-that's unbelievable," she said hesitantly.

"You need to listen to this," I whispered.

She sniffled quietly, listening to the story.

I spoke softly to her. "I'm not going to cut open your cocoon, but I will be here with you as you struggle through this, and I can't wait to watch you fly."

I told the woman with father pain about the post-abortive woman and how much her email had impacted her that day. I shared that I needed to find a chrysalis for the post-abortive woman, having no idea where to look for one. The memorial for her child was scheduled to be in eight weeks.

"I can get you one! I get them every year for my kids!" she exclaimed.

She and another lady prayed over the cocoons before she gave one for the post-abortive woman, plus one for each member of my family. We all needed to see something that appeared dead come back to life.

What were the chances that the butterfly would emerge from its chrysalis on the day of the memorial? She received it a few weeks ahead of time. I could not begin to even calculate what the odds were. In fact, when she said she was praying for the timing of the butterfly emerging, I said nothing, thinking, *You'd better prepare for disappointment because the chances of that butterfly emerging that day are the same as us flying to the moon.*

The day of the memorial came. She invited family members and had it in a very particular place; at the gravesite of her aborted child's father. He had passed away a few years before.

We agreed to meet at the cemetery's gates. It was interesting that it was the same cemetery my mom's ashes were interred in. Driving to the city, a grey sky loomed with showers. They cleared as I reached the city. Following behind her vehicle as the winding paths led to the site, memories of my mom's death and interment were coming back to life.

As I followed, she stopped her car in the same area of Mom's gravesite. She walked slowly to the gravesite. It was right by Mom's. How could that be? How could that happen?

She pulled out a container. It contained the most beautiful butterfly I had ever seen. Its wings appeared to glow. "When did it come out?" I gasped.

Tears streamed down her face as she answered, "An hour ago."

After we praised and worshiped God, and after she finished honoring her child, it was time to go. The butterfly was still there when we left, honoring the renewed faith that emerged in everyone who was present that day.

LIFE LESSON #36: People can stay in a protective cocoon, but when it's their season for healing, it's important to face the struggle. It might be painful and might take a while, but they will be stronger because of it. God may want to use them to help others, and it may be the time He wants them to unfurl their wings and fly.

Upon finishing her struggle through the father pain program, the woman who gave me the cocoons wrote: *A light has been switched on. It's not dark anymore, ugly, yes, but not scary. In fact, the light reveals that it isn't an abyss, but a tunnel that I have to go through to discover who I am and to get me to where God wants me to be!*

Fatherlessness is the meristem tissue of a tremendous amount of the emotional, physical, mental, relational, and spiritual burdens in our society. If it's never dealt with, people can pass all the abortion laws they long for, but the unplanned pregnancies will keep occurring.

CHAPTER 47

As our car meandered down the highway, during a trip to the mountains, I noticed a kayak serenely floating on the river. My heart leaped. I checked out the possibility of renting one when we reached our destination. The next day, I had never felt such peace as I experienced kayaking for the first time. It had now become a passion. I purchased my own kayak, and God and I spent much time alone together on the water. He continually revealed Himself through it. I came to love kayaking, so much that it wasn't long before I purchased a higher quality one.

One day, I did something I'd never done before with a client. I challenged a woman who was working through the father pain program to go kayaking with me.

It had not been easy for her to turn and face the pain that had been chasing her. Kayaking was something she had never experienced before and she eagerly accepted the invitation. But I wondered if I was doing the right thing by allowing someone into my private world outside the center.

After some basic instruction, we started our way up the river. I told her I always go "up" the river first, against the current, then out onto the lake. "It will be a struggle for you to make it to the lake, but trust me, once you get there, it will be worth it," I assured her. "Follow me and you will be okay."

As we made our way up the river, the usual undercurrents attempted to turn our kayaks sideways. I had warned her of them before we started. "You must paddle hard and strong to keep your kayak straight when the undercurrent hits," I said. "It's one of the ways God has revealed Himself to me, telling me that as I travel the path with Him, things will happen to try to tow me away, but I must keep my eyes ahead and paddle strong. I cannot control the current. All I can do is try to control my own kayak."

After paddling under bridges, through a dam, and stopping once to rest, we finally made it to the lake. "You will notice a change in the water. Your kayak will feel more buoyant."

I explained to her earlier how being on the lake made me feel. "I have been on the lake when the water is so calm it's like glass, and I've been on the lake when the waves are so high, the front of my kayak goes up in the air, and then slams into the water. But I am never afraid. My subconscious mind compares it to being in my mother's womb; safe, secure, protected, no matter what the circumstances. And I am never alone."

A perfectly calm day, we made our way further out onto the lake. "Are there any fish in this lake?" she asked.

"Oh yes! In fact, I have sometimes seen small schools of them feeding with their mouths open just above the water."

Within five minutes, a school of fish appeared just above the water line, hungry, and feeding. Soon, hundreds surrounded our kayaks, as far as eyes could see. Many of them close enough that if we had a net, we could scoop them up. "I have never seen this," I whispered as I looked with wonder. Her eyes were as big as saucers.

Somehow, I could sense this woman would mentor other women. It was clear to me that God had a calling on her life. "God is talking to you," I said. "He is showing you the number of people you will help if you stay on this course with Him."

She looked overwhelmed. "I'm not sure if I can help all of those people."

I told her about an incident that had occurred two weeks earlier. A friend and I had attended a conference near the ocean. Each night after the sessions, we walked to the beach and watched the waves rolling into the shore, each pondering what we learned that day.

One evening, as we sat on the beach my heart was overwhelmed, thinking of the world's pain. Tears formed, and I closed my eyes, hoping the sound of the waves would wash the feeling away. It didn't.

I felt very defeated. What was the point in helping anyone anymore? "There are too many," I said silently to God. "I can't do this anymore, Lord. It's too much. I want to quit and go home."

When I opened my eyes, a fisherman appeared to the right of us on the beach. But this wasn't just any fisherman. He fished with a net. I had never seen this kind of fishing before. It was high tide, and he threw one end of the net into the ocean and anchored the other end securely on shore. His partner stood and watched him.

After throwing the net into the ocean, he and his partner sat and waited. Half an hour later, he waded into the ocean, clad in hip waders, a pouch around his neck to collect any fish that might be in the net. "Wow!" we heard him yell, "This is my biggest catch ever!"

I turned to my friend, tears running down my cheeks. "Oh, is God ever talking," I lamented. "Here I am, thinking I can't handle the amount of emotional pain of the world and God is saying, 'Melony, I'm not asking you to help the whole world. That's My job. I'm asking you to cast a net where I tell you to and to help the ones I put into it.'"

The woman sat in her kayak next to me, hanging on every word I told her. I remembered letting out a long sigh, closing my eyes, and thanking God while the fisherman excitedly chatted with his partner as another wave washed up on shore. She understood.

It was time to head back down the river. As the current guided us along, I silently thanked God for placing her in the Options center's net.

CHAPTER 48

In the spring of 2015, I approached Jodie with an idea. I had become good friends with Julie, who had taken the father pain program and attended the conference near the ocean with me. She had four children whom she home-schooled. Originally from South Africa, it was her and her husband's dream to save money and one day take their children to Africa for a year. Now the dream had come true. They were working at an orphanage in Africa, the orphanage run by Ranji who had invited me to see it in 2009.

At one point while in Africa, one of their son's arms was injured, so Julie flew back to Canada with him for a couple of weeks for medical reasons. During that time, she visited me at the center and said I should bring my family, including the boys, over to Africa.

"Oh, no Julie, that will NEVER happen," I had said, matter-of-factly. I did not want to go to Africa. I did not enjoy long plane rides. I did not like being away from home for more than a few days. I did not like the disruption. The list went on.

My mouth said *never*, but God worked on my heart. Through the winter, the thought kept coming back. It would be the perfect opportunity to allow my grandsons' hearts to mend somewhat, with other children who also had lost one or both parents. I felt that God had a calling on one or more of the boys' lives.

So now, I told Jodie the idea, but first I shared with her something that had happened the previous weekend. The boys and I were talking about Julie and her family and what they were doing in Africa. I explained that they saved their money for a long time to volunteer at the orphanage for a year.

"Why would someone want to work for nothing?" Alex piped up.

"Money is not the most important thing in the world, Alex. What do you think is?"

He answered immediately, "My life."

I softly responded, "You're wrong. It's God. And if your dad hadn't believed in God, we would not know where he is."

A big smile came across Jodie's face as I shared the conversation. She said they hadn't been able to go to church that weekend and Alex had been disappointed. Now she realized why.

After explaining the idea of a trip to Africa, I thought Jodie might think I had lost my mind. With great tenderness, I looked at her and asked, "Will you go?"

As tears welled in her eyes she said, "Mom, I think it's a great idea."

Now that Jodie was on board, we could not imagine going without Lindsey. The fall of the previous year, the girls and I had traveled together to Greece and Italy. "Mom, what are people going to think?" Lindsey asked. I asked her what she wanted to be, a people pleaser, or a God pleaser. She chose the latter and within two weeks, tickets were purchased.

I had no idea what we would do when we got there other than spend lots of time with the orphans, but I did know it would mean so much more if the boys could fundraise and help with a project. When I asked Julie about it, she said there wasn't much for the orphans to do at the orphanage. She said there were scooters in the shed, but there was nowhere to ride them. So I sent Ranji an email and asked what she thought of pouring a basketball court size cement pad for the kids to skateboard on, ride scooters on, and play basketball. She loved it.

The projected cost was $1,300 in U.S. funds, so the next weekend, Jodie sent me a text with a picture. The boys had set up a juice stand in front of the house to raise funds. My heart leapt and my eyes filled with tears as I realized God was working, and we hadn't even left yet.

Within a few days, I messaged back and forth with Julie. She told me of two incidents with the orphans, but one in particular caught my attention. A five-year-old girl lived at the orphanage and one day, a volunteer brought a cake. It happened to be the little girl's birthday. They called all the kids in and sang happy birthday to her, completely sure the little girl would be thrilled. They were wrong. She burst into uncontrollable sobs. Julie was confused as to the problem.

"I think I know what happened," I said. "Would you sub-consciously like to celebrate the day you were separated from your mother?" The light bulb illuminated. That night I wrote an email to Ranji asking her what she thought of me bringing the adoptee program to the orphanage.

"Yes!" she wrote, "Anything that will help our children."

And that was that. The die was cast. We had no idea what was to happen, but God had clearly asked, "Will you go?" We said, "Yes."

Just before we left for Africa, I gave the last of seven school presentations which were scheduled over a two-week period. The last one was in a lab with sixty kids. I thought to myself, *This will not work. No one will hear me in this room!* But you could've heard a pin drop during the presentation. I spoke of a picture I posted on Facebook of a snake coming out of a body of water with a fish in its mouth. The caption on the picture read, "Brave snake saves drowning fish." I told them not to be deceived; this is exactly what Satan wanted them to think. He wants them to stay in their pain and to be comfortable with it.

I also shared that my family was going to Africa and how so many people approached us, fearing for our lives. Ebola had killed numerous people in Africa. "What about Ebola? What about Aids? What about Isis?" they asked, so I told the kids a lesson I once learned. It was simply this: If we always give in to fear, we will get nothing done!

Afterward, one teacher said to the other, "Don't forget to check the door in the back because that rabbit keeps getting out."

"Rabbit?" I asked.

"Oh yes!" she said. "There's a rabbit back there and there's a snake in another container." I couldn't believe my ears. It was as though the evil one had physically manifested himself right there in the classroom, letting me know he was watching. But I know I don't have to fear him. I have Someone greater than him on my side.

LIFE LESSON #37: *If we keep giving in to the fears we have,*
    NOTHING will ever get done.

CHAPTER 49

Soon after we arrived to the orphanage, work started on the cement pad. It would serve as a basketball court at the orphanage. We pitched in to help, doing everything by manual labor. But the cement pad was not the focus.

Dwayne and Julie introduced us to the children. Once my

grandsons got over their shyness, they started interacting with them. For me and my daughters, it was a different story.

As soon as the wee ones saw us "mzungus," they immediately came toward us with arms outstretched; desperately trying to do whatever it took to fill their very empty emotional cups with just a few drops of love.

Our hearts broke. We were strangers in a strange land, but they did not see us in that light. Every day, I saw what I had come to know. If a child's emotional cup is not being filled, they will try to extract it from anyone around them, including the aliens in their midst. They did not sense any danger. They saw a body with two arms, arms that could be put around them, arms that could melt away the growing hardness in their hearts.

It bothered me that they did not care who we were or whether we posed any danger to them or their fragile hearts, but we tried to give as much love as possible. They pushed each other out of the way, the light quickly extinguishing in their eyes when they weren't one of the ones to be picked up.

The night before I was to speak in the chapel, I asked Austin if I could have a private conversation with him. We went into the bedroom and he picked up a ball and started throwing it against the wall, letting it bounce back to the floor, his quick reflexes catching it to do it over and over again. Part of me wanted to take him by the shoulders and say, "Austin, I'm talking to you!" But I kept my mouth shut, knowing he needed to keep himself busy. He knew this would be one of "those" conversations.

We talked of everything that had transpired; the sights and sounds of the beautiful, strange land. It was then time for the tough part of the conversation. The pace of the ball hitting the wall quickened.

We talked about the pain and anger that had entered his heart and life when Aaron passed away in the motorcycle accident. Then I asked him if he would allow me to speak of the pain he had been going through with the children of the orphanage at the Sunday service the next morning. It might help them. He didn't answer.

I asked if he felt a connection with the children. A puzzled look crossed over his face and said, "Yeah, Grandma, I do."

I asked if he understood why. He could not think of any reason. I asked if it was the fact that the children at the orphanage had also lost one or more parents. The light bulb went on.

The children there never talked of their pain, but Austin knew it was important to share. If his pain was shared, it might help them see their own.

"Grandma, if you think it will help them, then I think you should share it."

LIFE LESSON #38: *God will use our pain to help others if we allow Him.*

> *Blessed be the God and Father of our Lord Jesus Christ,*
> *the Father of mercies and God of all comfort,*
> *who comforts us in all our affliction so that we will be*
> *able to comfort those who are in any affliction with the*
> *comfort with which we ourselves are comforted by God.*
> 2 CORINTHIANS 1:3–4

The next day, as I shared the hammer story and the impact it had on my life, my eyes met Austin's. It was time to share about his pain.

Alex and Ronan had left the chapel to go to Sunday school with the other kids from the orphanage. Jodie had her arm around Austin, helping him move through the wave of pain she knew would hit. His eyes fixated on the floor, his feelings desperately tried to find a firm place to touch bottom as his spirit struggled to breathe above the ocean of pain. He shuddered as the tears—that God cared so much for—spilled their way onto his cheeks as I spoke. It was a mark on his road of healing and it was a mark on the road of healing to those who shared his pain.

I ended by telling the snake story and how they should not be deceived—Satan wants no one to move through their pain. After the service had ended, we stood outside the chapel. Julie's husband, Dwayne, came running up to us excitedly with a pail.

"Look at what was behind the boys' house!"

In the bottom of the pail, was a deadly snake that had just been killed. My eyes popped out of my head.

Satan was still watching.

CHAPTER 50

That night, the thirteen to eighteen-year-olds at the orphanage started the adoptee program. They had listened to a portion of my story that morning in the chapel, and I told them the program was based on the story of Moses.

Julie and a couple of other adults from the orphanage sat in on it. A few of them opened up that night and spoke. One of the most profound things that came out of that evening was the subject of triggers—things that subconsciously cue us into the traumas that have occurred in our lives, tapes that make the emotional trauma play over and over in our heads.

I talked about some of my triggers, one of them being called an adoptee and the anger I felt when hearing the term. The kids recognized the profound impact of one of their own triggers—being called an orphan. When they heard the term, it reminded them of what they were. I thought of the terms "Miss" or "Mrs." It predicates our names to let people know what our status is regarding being married or unmarried. But this was different. They said even at the schools they attended, when someone introduced them, they would end the introduction with, "He/ She is an orphan," as though that summed up everything they were.

One of them talked of the feelings he experienced when people found out he was an orphan. "I can see the look in their eyes change," he said, "and it sickens me."

Austin had spoken about the same feeling when someone would find out his father had died. It was as though the event summed up whom they were, for the rest of their lives.

All of us were impacted that night as tears fell. They did not want to be loved because of *what* they were. They wanted to be loved for *who* they were.

The next night, the adults who hadn't been there the previous night sat in plus a couple more. The kids weren't opening up the way they did the first night. It was obvious that a level of trust had been established the night before. When the adults heard about how the kids had opened up, it was only natural that they wanted to see for themselves. But I could sense what the kids felt. I wanted to yell, "What are you doing here? These are not laboratory rats that are here for observation! These are human beings with hearts and souls!" But I said nothing.

Julie and I were the only adults present the next night. "Before anyone else shows up, I want to ask you something. Last night, I sensed you did not open up the way you did the previous night. Is it because of the adults present?" They nodded vehemently in answer.

"I'm not a leader here at the orphanage, but I will see what I can do to ensure no other adults show up." Miraculously, no other adult showed up that night or any of the nights to come.

I shared more about my life with them, including the

abortion. They shared even more of the things they experienced. My heart and Julie's were breaking inside for them.

One of them talked about the impact of the program. "I have a classmate who lives at another orphanage and who is in pain. I told him about this program and how much he needs to go through it!" Another boy wanted to speak with me when the group finished for the night. I gasped as he spoke of the traumatic details of his past. "Please help me," he shuddered as he cried.

Another young man waited outside. I thought he was waiting for the boy I had been talking with. He wasn't. "I want you to know something," he said as tears fell. "I have never talked about any of what I have been through before. Tonight was the first time." I hugged him and expressed how God wanted to bring him through all of it.

As I laid in bed staring at the ceiling thinking about what my ears had heard, I thanked God for everything He had brought me through, and for bringing me to this place.

The last night, I encouraged them to continue going through the program after I was gone. We talked about who could lead them through it and I asked them who they would be comfortable with. I knew what their answer was before I asked the question.

"Would you like me to ask one of the managers, or perhaps the social worker?" They shook their heads no.

It had nothing to do with the manager or the social worker personally; it had to do with how they viewed someone regarding their position or level of authority. The orphanage was the place that clothed, housed, and fed them. They would be afraid of doing something or saying something to jeopardize that, in particular, saying something to someone who represented authority with the orphanage. They would not want to bite the hand that fed them. The authority figure could tell them nothing would happen and they could be open with their emotions, but it was an authority figure, (their parents), that "left" them before, hence the reason for going through the program in the first place.

"Would you feel safe with Julie?" They nodded.

Julie agreed to lead them through the next part of the program before she and her family left in the next couple of months.

CHAPTER 51

One of the orphanage managers felt strongly that I should speak with the head mistress of one of the more prestigious schools about creating an environment of trust so girls at the school would come forward to the leaders in the school to share their pain; so started another memorable day.

The head mistress set up a meeting with the teachers and two of the prefects (student leaders) for the school. I shared about my life and about the environment we strive to set at the center to allow people to expose their pain.

The principal asked if I would share my story with the Grade 11 and 12 girls, two hundred in all. Quickly, (which is not typical for the African culture,) the presentation was set up. They reacted the same way the students reacted the previous time I had been in Africa. They were elated that someone was speaking truth to their hearts. I was reminded again that it doesn't matter what race, color, religion, or economic status you are, if you have pain, it affects people the same way.

When I finished my presentation, Dwayne, Julie, Jodie, Lindsey, and the boys met me and we went to a place I previously expressed an interest in going to—the Victoria Falls Bridge, one of the most beautiful spots in the world to bungee jump from.

I thought I would be able to change my clothes, but there we were at the bridge with me in my "speaking" clothes, trying to determine whether I wanted to jump. Standing for what seemed an eternity, I peered into the gorge at the churning river. I asked my family for their opinion. Should I jump? Jodie didn't have a problem with it. The boys thought it was very cool. Lindsey was not in favor and later confessed, "Mom, I was so afraid of losing you!" But I sensed something pushing me to do it.

As they were putting the gear on me, Lindsey was in tears. Alex looked like he was afraid. They were both praying. The workers asked me if I was scared. I replied, "A little, but nothing major." As they placed what appeared to be a life jacket over my head, they asked if I could swim. I replied, *yes*, I could indeed swim. I put my arms out as they instructed me in the "I'm about to jump off this bridge pose." There was no fear, no trembling, nothing.

Then I jumped. My eyes were open the whole time. I didn't scream, nothing. After the first jerk of the rope, I looked around in total awe. I felt fantastic! What a rush!

Two weeks later at home, I did a lot of processing. I said to Lawrence, "There's something about that jump. Just after I decided to do it, I got this feeling. It did not go away as they put the gear on me. It was not a foreign feeling, I've felt it before."

Never had I done anything like this before, yet I recognized the feeling. I had disassociated myself from my emotions. I had become a robot. I had numbed myself. I felt nothing. It was the exact same feeling before the abortion thirty years before.

God multitasked in so many ways on the trip, but He wanted me to come face to face once again with the experience. He spoke to my heart. "Melony, I'm so glad you recognized the emotion. From now on, when you are in a place of feeling nothing, I want you to know it is not from Me. I wanted to take you *through* the sensation so you sense even stronger the intense joy I have for you on the other side of it."

I recognized if you can't feel intense pain then you won't feel intense joy either. I have never felt more alive than I did at that moment. And I could tell it wasn't the adrenaline rush—it was God.

After the jump, as I had walked back still clad in the bungee gear, someone said, "What's that tab on your life jacket?"

Before I could respond that I didn't know, someone else said, "That's the tab you pull to inflate it if you need it."

No one instructed me how to inflate the life jacket before I jumped.

LIFE LESSON #39: *People do painful, traumatic things or painful, traumatic things are done to them. Many do not recognize they have God's life jacket on, and they end up in a place of "nothingness," unaware that there is a tab on the life jacket they can pull.*

CHAPTER 52

A couple of days before we left Africa, Austin became ill, very ill. And I would be lying if I said the thought of Ebola didn't cross my mind. In fact, the thoughts relentlessly pierced my brain. "Way to go, Melony. You put your family at risk, and now look at what's happening." I prayed fervently. And I drank heavily.

Julie called Ranji's husband, Dr. Chara, in the middle of the night to come see Austin. Austin was promptly diagnosed with tonsillitis, which he had never had before, and was given an injection of antibiotic, which according to him, was with the biggest needle ever. We chuckled as we told him everything was big in Africa.

On the way home, the airports still had "fever meters" due to the Ebola outbreak and Austin did everything possible to appear healthy so we could make it through. He did not want to be responsible for us being quarantined and not arriving home on schedule. This sense of being responsible appeared abnormally high. I noted it for a future conversation.

We made it back to Canada, but we still had an eight-hour drive during the night to make it home. It was May 30, 2015.

As you recall, on May 30, 2013, I wrote: *Father, Son, and Holy Spirit, I choose You, Lord. I choose to feel comfort in the safety of Your arms. I choose to not feel anxious about Your love, Lord. I feel like I have been running my whole life. And I feel like I have been trying to wear other people's armor throughout the battles in my life. You have been standing there with the right one this whole time, waiting for me to fall from sheer exhaustion so that You could put it on me. I choose to have the most intimate relationship and friendship with You, Lord. I went for a walk on Sunday. I have been feeling as though You have been preparing me for future battles. As I was walking, I started noticing various rocks. I picked up different ones, remembering the five smooth stones David picked up to slay Goliath. After throwing some back down and picking up better ones, I ended up with five in my pocket. When I got home, it was as though I had an instant download from You. You told me that I had walked through my adoptee pain so that I would fully understand who I am, but especially who I am in You. And that I needed to know this so that I will be comfortable wearing the armor You have given me for the future battles that lie ahead. The stones are on my desk at home. Thank You, Lord. I love You.*

I had brought the rocks with me on our trip. The sun was coming up as we drove. I sat in the exact place in the vehicle I had been sitting on the way home in the middle of the night that Aaron died. And so was Jodie.

I removed the rocks from my bag and explained them to my grandsons. I gave one to Lindsey. I gave one to Jodie. I gave one to Austin. I gave one to Alex. I gave one to Ronan.

God wanted to give them something physical to slay their emotional and spiritual Goliath of pain, and to slay all of their future Goliaths. He wanted them to know He was with them.

CHAPTER 53

We started the Circle of Security Parenting Program at the center. It was the program Julie and I had been trained on at the conference by the ocean, when God had placed the fisherman before me with the net.

An evening group started. After seeing the advertisement for the upcoming group at the center, an adoptive and foster mother had decided it might be worthwhile. Not for herself, but for the birth mother of one of her foster children who was trying desperately to get her child back. She decided the birth mother might benefit from a program like this. I chuckled to myself when she said she took the program so the birth mother could be helped. God lured her with that, but as usual, He was multi-tasking. It reminded me of when I decided to search for Peter, thinking I would do something to help him, not me.

The program spoke, not only to the heart of the birth mother of the foster child, but to hers. She learned that many times, when a child misbehaves, the cause is often rooted in how safe and secure they feel.

Children are looking for attachment and connection, and she understood her parenting was influenced by how she, herself, was parented, and by the trauma she experienced in her life.

One of the most important things you can do for a child is to show them how to go *through* their emotions, and not dance around them, and to *be with* them as they do so, otherwise the emotion will surface in another way. In our Western culture, we tend to do anything to deter someone from crying or showing anger.

One day, not the foster child, but her young, adopted son, approached her. Out of the blue, he asked, "Mom, why didn't my mommy want me?"

She stopped in her tracks, not expecting the question. She immediately stopped what she was doing and sat with him, tenderly and softly explaining that his birth mother didn't think she could take care of him adequately.

Moments passed. He looked into her eyes, the sorrow in his heart unmasking itself, and asked, "Why couldn't she take classes on how to be a mom like you are?"

She said she didn't know. He started to weep, and within a few minutes, sobs wracked his small body. She held him close as the sorrow continued to pour.

It took everything to fight against her mother's instinct to stop his tears, to distract him away from his emotions. But she learned through the program that stopping the tears does not stop the pain. As parents, we want to immediately place Band-Aids on our children's scrapes and kiss them better. But there was no Band-Aid big enough for this emotional wound. She must let the sadness "bleed out." She couldn't take his pain away, but she could "be with" him through it.

His sobs subsided, but only for a moment until another wave crashed against him. She said nothing, but her actions were loud and clear. (As he grew older, the wound would reopen and close, reopen and close, but she no longer felt threatened or scared or overwhelmed by his wound. She embraced it.) She held him until the storm passed, and she could see a rainbow of hope appear as his tears abated. Then he got up and went outside to play.

It was a moment she would never forget. It was a moment that anchored his connection and trust in her. He felt safe with her, safe enough to let out his emotion and his pain.

It was a moment that would anchor his trust in Christ Emmanuel, God is with us.

CHAPTER 54

I had a wish. I knew I would share the hammer story with people, but I prayed it would be on Father's Day. I ended up sharing about my abortion on Mother's Day; in the very city it had taken place thirty years earlier. If God could set that up, He would set up Father's Day.

I shared the story with a pastor in the city. He asked if I would share it with his congregation. He said there were two openings coming up, Father's Day and one in September, and asked me to pray about which date it should be. I didn't need to pray. God set it up, and it happened.

Lawrence, Jodie, and the boys attended. I saw many tears throughout the congregation as I shared the story of the hammers. I shared about the children at the orphanage. I shared my grandsons' pain. And all along, I knew God was doing emotional heart surgery on selected people that day.

Afterward, Jodie wanted to take us out for lunch, to honor Lawrence, her stepfather, for Father's Day. Austin, Alex, and Ronan were getting impatient as people continued to talk with me after the service. The boys poked their heads around the corner, "Grandma, are you done yet?"

I laughed and said I just had to grab my purse. Alex could hardly contain himself. I thought it was because he was hungry, but he had something to share.

"Grandma, guess what?" he said excitedly. "Austin got into a fight in school on Friday and was suspended for a day!"

I gazed at Austin. "Still working on getting rid of that anger, huh?"

Alex and Ronan hurt just as bad, but Austin's anger was there for everyone to see, complete with a black eye, as he had received what he had dished out.

We didn't discuss it again that day. Tucking it away, I asked Jodie if I could take Austin kayaking that Monday.

"Yes, you can take him, Mom, as long as he doesn't think he's being rewarded for what happened," she answered.

As usual, we ventured up the river, against the current first. I had never taken him that far. It was clear he wanted to prove himself, and he made it.

As we floated back, we talked about what happened. I explained what a trigger was, and he understood immediately. "Oh, just like a gun, Grandma? A trigger sets someone off?"

"Exactly," I replied. "Do you think there was a trigger the day you got into the fight?"

He couldn't think of anything.

"Do you think a certain day was approaching, that might have set you off?"

The light bulb went on. "Father's Day," he said, lowering his eyes.

We talked about anger again and how good and necessary it is that we feel it, that it is an important part of the grieving process, but that God says in His word it is important no one else be hurt as we let it out.

I smiled as he reminded me I still hadn't bought the punching bag I promised to buy them; the punching bag that Jodie said she could use as well. Then I took a chance, a big one. I had a strong sense Austin felt something significant about Aaron's death.

"Austin, I want to talk with you about one more thing. I think you feel responsible for your dad's death."

He looked at me quizzically as we continued to float side by side down the river. "I don't understand what you're saying, Grandma." I knew he understood perfectly, but he needed to deflect so that what was said would ease into his spirit instead of bombarding it.

With great care, I said, "I think you think if you wouldn't have gone to your friend's place to stay overnight, your dad would not have gone out on that motorcycle ride and he would still be alive today."

He turned away so I couldn't see the tears spilling down his face. The words hung there, in the air, waiting to see which direction to go, finally settling. Then came the response I knew in my heart was there.

"I think that all day. Every day," he said. He almost choked on the words. He was only eleven years old.

I closed my eyes, preparing my mind for what he needed to hear as I steered our kayaks to a stop in the reeds at the side of the river. I took off my sunglasses and asked him to look into my eyes. He did so, reluctantly. "Austin, you are not responsible for your father's death. Everyone has a day they are born and everyone has a day they die. You don't get to pick."

I cried as I continued. "I've told you before; it's okay to be angry with God. He has big shoulders. You *will* get through this, and you *will* be stronger than most people because of it. I know it sucks right now. But I'm here for you. I love you. Your mom is here for you. She loves you. But there is Someone who loves you far more than your mom and I put together. Do you know who it is?"

"Yeah," he sobbed, "it's God."

CHAPTER 55

Lawrence's sister died quickly. Headaches plagued her, and she was not feeling well a few weeks before. Previously, she had fought breast cancer, but the doctors could not pinpoint what was now happening in her body.

She was admitted into the hospital on a Wednesday. We saw her Thursday afternoon. The following Monday, she was diagnosed with stage-four cancer throughout her body. By Tuesday, she was gone.

The day before her funeral, I received a call that Peter's ashes were being sent in the mail. Lawrence called me at the center to tell me the "package" was at the post office. Peter had arrived.

The parcel came via regular parcel post. I didn't even have to sign for it. I asked the postmistress if she knew what was in the package. "Well, I thought it was seeds or something like that. I turned it over and shook it but I realized it was too heavy to be seeds."

The package came from the university Peter donated his body to for research. It was now three years later. The postmistress was shocked when I told her what was in the package. I told her the short version of the story and she started to tear up. She found out a few years earlier she had an older brother who was placed for adoption.

I put the box in the front seat and put my arm protectively over it whenever I came to a stop sign. Lawrence was standing there, holding the door open, when I got home and ushered me in. I opened the brown-paper wrapped package. It was sealed heavily with tape. His ashes were in a white cardboard box with his name printed on a white label on the side. This was a man made in God's image who donated his body for the good of mankind, and his remains were sent via regular post mail, in a white cardboard box, wrapped in brown paper. I wasn't sure what I thought, but it didn't matter.

The same night Peter's ashes arrived, Lawrence and I sat outside. Suddenly, thousands and thousands of dragonflies flew above, about sixty feet in the air. Neither of us had ever witnessed something so amazing. I thought of the dragonfly story. Once the creature becomes an adult dragonfly, it cannot go back to its family and original earthly home in the pond. He must wait for them to join him.

God had been calling on me to have a service for Peter, to honor him once I received his ashes, but also to help others recognize their own "father pain." I thought I would receive them within a year of him passing away, but three years had passed, and I was thankful. Thankful because it took me three years to come to terms with what happened. I could now truly honor Peter.

I checked into dates to have the service. And then it hit me. Three years earlier on August 26th, I had used Peter's hammer to smash the heart of stone, my heart of stone. August 26th was Pearl's birthday. And exactly three years after I shattered the heart of stone, I would honor them both.

I asked my friend Julie's husband Dwayne, whom God had clearly called to be an earthly father to the fatherless, to construct Peter's urn. Dwayne was a carpenter, a good one, just like Peter had been. He constructed it out of weathered wood from our farm. It was beautiful.

I bought a bunch of butterfly stickers. The night of the service, I wanted to share the hammer story and the butterfly story, and invite anyone with father pain wanting to honor their fathers despite the pain, to step forward and place a butterfly on Peter's urn. God would use the process of having them do something physical, to start moving them through their emotional and spiritual pain.

Peter loved baseball, and the Blue Jays were his favorite team, so I walked into a store two days before the service to buy a Blue Jays jersey to wear at his memorial. Other customers sauntered about. A young woman asked if I needed help. I told her I was looking for a Blue Jays jersey. She said they had one and took me to that part of the store. I put it on and she said it looked great and asked if I wanted to look in a mirror. I said no, it was fine. Then she said they ordered a lot of them, but they only received one that morning. I became teary-eyed and as we walked to the cash register, I told her what a God thing this was that there was only one and that it came that morning. I told her my birth father was a big Blue Jays fan, and I wanted to wear the jersey to his service.

She looked at me and said, "Well then you will think it's even more of a God thing because we have been told that due to the Blue Jays doing so well in the standings, the demand for their jerseys is so high that we can't expect any for quite some time—if at all."

LIFE LESSON #40: *When you see God taking care of the little details in your life, you will be in even more awe when you see Him taking care of the big ones.*

The night before the service, I carefully wrapped Peter's ashes in a purple scarf. I recalled the profound experience it was, the first time I touched Peter's ashes through the bag. I was reminded of the conversation Julie and I had, when I showed them to her.

"It's not like ash at all," she whispered, "it's like sand. How can someone not believe God made us from sand after seeing this?"

The morning of the service, Lawrence asked if I wanted to

place anything in the urn before I closed it. Peter's wife had given me his wedding ring after he died. "I've been wearing Peter's ring on my index finger for three years. I wore it on my index finger because that's where I wore rings when I was a little girl, and it was the little girl inside of me that needed her daddy. It was the little girl inside of me that needed to heal."

And with that, as I wept, I tenderly tucked the ring inside the scarf beside his ashes.

CHAPTER 56

A few days earlier, the message indicator had sounded on my iPad. A couple I knew said a young woman wanted to place her child for adoption—with them—and they recommended she come into the center. For appearances sake, I would have to distance myself from this young woman. If she intended to place her child for adoption with someone I knew, even though it all happened before I even met the woman, it would not look good to outsiders. Surely, I could be a God pleaser and a people pleaser at the same time, right?

She came into the center and asked to speak with me specifically. *Great*, I thought to myself, *so much for keeping myself at a distance*. But I was sure that once I explained all of this to her, she would understand *my* need and would agree to talk with someone else at the center. Then I heard the young woman's story.

In my spirit, I named her Braveheart. She was a new Christian. In her culture, having a child out of wedlock would bring shame to her family. Her parents were arriving in the city within a few days to ensure she aborted. That was *their* plan. She had already canceled two abortion appointments. To please her family, she now made a third appointment to abort. But *her* plan was to place the child for adoption. And she wanted me to convince her parents. There I was, smack dab in the middle. My need to distance myself and be a people pleaser so I wouldn't offend anyone suddenly seemed insignificant.

Her parents were flying in the next Tuesday. She asked if I could meet with her parents the day after, which was Wednesday. *Interesting date,* I thought to myself. *The service for Peter will be that night.* The abortion appointment was scheduled for Friday, two days after Peter's memorial.

I explained to her there was little chance of convincing her parents she should place her child for adoption. Any attempt to change their minds would most likely be in vain. On top of it all, they did not speak English. She would have to interpret everything said—to them and to me. It seemed pointless, but she was at the end of her very short rope. I made the appointment.

As predicted, it did not matter what I said. They could not see past themselves at how this abortion would emotionally and spiritually hurt their daughter. "If she was in our country, my daughter would be dead," her father stated, matter-of-factly.

"But she is not in your country. She is in Canada."

I could see her spirit inflate as she interpreted to them what I was saying, then deflate as she interpreted back what they said. Inflate. Deflate. Inflate. Deflate. I saw the knife go into her spirit as she listened to what they said, and then she grimaced as it twisted and she was forced to repeat what they said in English. It was simple. They wanted her child dead, or the family would feel her shame.

They explained that Canada was far different from their country regarding a woman having a child out of wedlock. In turn, I explained the impact of my own unplanned pregnancy at fifteen. Not allowed to go to school, neighbours secretly brought over gifts for my child. Yes, today was far from what it looked like thirty-seven years ago.

Then I did something I rarely did. I showed them pictures of my two daughters and my three grandsons. They looked at them, tears forming in their eyes, but the hardness of their hearts forced the tears back.

I also did something strange that I felt led to do. The service for Peter would take place that night. I had placed the urn containing his ashes in the same room where I was speaking with the young woman's parents. They were not aware of it, yet.

I told them it had not been easy, but my parents, the ones who adopted me, were culture changers. I told them how my dad came into my room ten days after I placed my daughter for adoption and found me crying, how he said if it hurt this bad, I'd better keep her. My dad didn't care what others thought. He was a God pleaser, not a people pleaser. He was a culture changer.

I challenged them. I told them they too had the opportunity to be culture changers. But her father hung his head, saying, "I am not strong enough."

Her mother wept. "My father and mother did not live together when I was young," her daughter interpreted quickly as she spoke. "My husband's family still throws that in my face."

Her eyes grew wide when I looked at her and softly said, "You have father pain."

Her weeping continued when I said, "Do you see that box over there? It contains the ashes of the birth father who didn't care to be my father when I was born. My God has asked me to honor him, and I am having a service tonight to do just that."

They told their daughter they wanted to speak with her alone and got up to leave. We shook hands, and as they walked out of the room, I said to Braveheart, "Ask your mother if I can give her a hug." She did so, and her mother turned, sobbing, and hugged with everything she had.

"Please come to the service tonight," I said gently. They said they would.

They did not attend. But forty-five others did. Dwayne and his eldest son played worship music. I told the hammer story and talked about the pain my grandsons were going through. I told the butterfly story and then did what God lead me to do. I invited those with father pain, who wanted to step forward and honor their fathers in spite of the pain, to place a butterfly sticker on Peter's urn. It became covered with butterflies. And it was beautiful.

I had nailed the urn shut that morning, except for three nails. At the end of the service, I used the golden hammer to nail in the last three nails. It had never been used before that night.

Friday morning arrived, and I texted Braveheart to see how she was doing.

"Can I fake an abortion?" she texted back.

I told her to tell the people at the hospital what was happening. I told her if God was calling on her not to abort, then she should do whatever was necessary.

"We are heading to the hospital," she texted. The next text came fast. "Can I just run away?"

My heart in my throat, I texted, "If you need me to come and get you, I will. I can be there in an hour."

Could I find someone to hide her? I was messaging Julie at the same time and told her what was happening. I asked her to pray. "I'm at the hospital with my mom!" Julie messaged back, "I will watch out for her!"

"I ran away," said the next text from Braveheart. "I'm driving."

"Come to the center. I will hide you myself!"

"Ok," she texted.

Julie messaged back immediately saying she would leave the hospital to meet her. "Just tell her what I'm driving and I will meet her in the center's parking lot."

I texted Braveheart, praying she would meet her.

"Ok," she replied.

"Hang in there! I will be there as fast as I can," I texted. Driving like a maniac, I quickly pulled over, texting her again. "Are you with Julie yet?"

"Yes," she responded.

There she was, sitting in Julie's van, looking terrified and traumatized as I pulled into the parking lot. I took her into the center.

"I got into an argument with my parents first thing this morning," she said as she wept. "My dad told me, daughters like me are the reason some fathers kill their daughters."

Her friends and family started texting and calling within a short time, telling her she was being disrespectful to her parents. Never had I seen someone under this much pressure. "God is with you," I assured her. "He will protect you. You have made the right choice."

As we talked, she calmed down. I asked her to read some Scripture aloud. "Deuteronomy 30:19: This day I call the heavens and the earth as witnesses against you that I have set before you, life and death, blessings and curses. Now choose life, so that you and your children may live," she declared.

"Joshua 24:15: But if serving the Lord seems undesirable to you, then choose for yourselves this day whom you will serve, whether the gods your ancestors served beyond the Euphrates, or the gods of the Amorites, in whose land you are living. But as for me and my household, we will serve the Lord," she spoke boldly.

I told her *she* would be a culture changer. I told her how proud I was of her. She wept.

I found her a place to stay for the night and asked another couple if they would hide her for a while, until her parents left the country. They agreed. She was astounded how people were stepping up to the plate.

"Your culture is tightly woven," I said, "but so are we Christians."

A friend of hers came to the center to encourage her further, and to drive with her to where she would stay for the night. We opened the door gingerly; checking to make sure everything was safe and secure.

The next day things unravelled quickly. A member of her family convinced her to return to her parents. They said her parents would now accept the pregnancy.

I was extremely skeptical. The whole time, her father refused to speak with her, and her mother continued to cry and tell her she needed to abort.

In the meantime, something was happening. Braveheart was miscarrying. She was devastated. A few days later, she found out the child was dead in her womb before her parents even arrived in the country.

Julie and I could not believe what was happening. "Why would God have all of that happen knowing the child was already dead?" Julie lamented. I did not understand why.

Braveheart's parents were leaving the next week. She was broken. I texted her, "One of the Psalms says, 'I am shattered . . . like a broken dish . . .'"

She replied that her mother just kept crying, and she wished her father were more humble. They had planned to come to Peter's service but people had come over so they could not attend. Something kept stirring in my spirit about Braveheart's mother. I asked if she would be willing to bring her mother into the center. She agreed, and they came in.

The light was gone from Braveheart's eyes. I shared the hammer story with her mother as she interpreted. Her mother shared about the mistreatment she suffered as a child at the hands of her father.

I asked her if she felt God was there for her. She replied, "No."
I asked if I could tell her about *my* God. A spark of hope ignited
in her mother's eyes as I told her about everything He had done
for me. Braveheart gazed at me, clearly excited about the direction the conversation was going.

"He wants to be your God too. He's knocking on your door.
He is a gentleman and He will not come in unless He's asked.
Would you like to do that?"

"Yes," she said, as she nodded her head, tears streaming.

I asked her to repeat after me. And as her daughter interpreted, she repeated everything. Jesus Christ became *her* Lord
and Savior.

That Sunday, Braveheart took her parents to church. And as
she read her Bible that night, the father who, just days before,
told her she was the reason some fathers killed their daughters,
encouraged her to keep reading. Her unborn child was gone, but
there was new life after all.

Peter's ashes were interred in his hometown that Saturday
with many of his family members in attendance. I placed his
urn in the ground myself, and told everyone God had led me
to honor Peter, but in turn, God drew me closer to Himself.
I prayed my life, and the life of my daughters and grandsons,
would honor Peter and honor God.

Everything had come full circle.

CHAPTER 57

Various people continued to come into the center, and I continued to see "father pain" as a recurring theme. Two couples
stood out.

A young woman came in. She was at a five on the scale of one to ten of whether she wanted to abort or not. It was clear her boyfriend was pushing her to abort. It also became clear, as she connected the dots during the appointment that she was in the same position her mother had been in when pregnant with her.

I asked if her parents were together and she said they were together. She had a great relationship with them. In the years I had been director, only two women who came to the center with unplanned pregnancies, had great relationships with their parents who were still married. Both women chose to have their babies. Yet, here she was with an unplanned pregnancy and a boyfriend who did not react well. I asked her if her boyfriend would be open to coming into the center with her. She brought him in the next day.

The wonderful father she referred to was her stepfather. She never met her biological father. She called him the "sperm donor." My insides cringed as she said the words.

Turning to her boyfriend, I asked, "Are you a Christian?"

"Yeah, I think I am, sort of. I go to church once a year."

"Do you trust God?"

"Yes, I trust Him, but I believe He gives us choices."

"What's your opinion of abortion?"

"I think it's okay, particularly when the girl is fourteen or fifteen years old."

My insides cringed, again. I asked him what his age was; already knowing he was much older than that. During the whole appointment, he emotionally and psychologically pushed her to abort.

"What about all the plans we've made?" he lamented to her. "Our life will be over unless you abort."

"Do you love her?" I asked.

"Oh, yes!" he exclaimed.

Knowing she wanted to have the child, I asked if he would be there for her if she chose to go through with the pregnancy. He said he would be there for her either way, but his tone and body language suggested otherwise.

"What do you think she would do, if you told her you love her so much you would do whatever it takes for her to have this child?"

He flung himself back against the chair and said sarcastically, "She would probably have the kid."

She sat there, stunned, his true colors coming to the surface vividly for all to see.

"And what would you do if he told you he would do whatever it takes?"

She hung her head, her body heaved with emotion. "I would have the child."

"What is your relationship like with your parents?" I asked him.

His face reddened and tears rose from remote places within him and spilled onto his face, as he angrily tried to wipe them away.

"Are your parents together?" I asked as I handed him some tissues.

"No," he said sullenly. He lived with his mother and stepfather. His biological father abandoned the family when he was small. "My biological father is a worthless piece of shit!" he said, as he wiped more tears.

I asked him if he knew what she called her biological father. He didn't, so I told him she called him the "sperm donor."

And once again, I told the story of my life, just as I had told her the day before. He was moved—sort of. He cried all over again and continued to tell her he would be there for her either way, but abortion was ultimately the best decision for them.

"Will you be resentful if she follows through with the pregnancy?"

"I would get over it," he replied, his body language once again screaming at the top of its lungs otherwise.

I waited a few moments and then asked him the question I knew needed to be asked. "Do you think your father is resentful of you?"

He closed his eyes. As his face reddened, and as his crying grew into sobs, he angrily grabbed a tissue from the box and sputtered, "I don't know. And I don't care!"

"You have a choice as to how resentful you will be. You clearly hold the power in this situation," I responded softly. "You have told the woman you claim to love you want her to abort your child. If she has this child, your son or daughter will end up calling you a sperm donor, a worthless piece of shit, or you can change history from repeating itself."

As they walked out, the weight on her heart was taking its toll. "I will be in contact with you soon," she promised. The abortion had already been scheduled for the next week. I had a feeling this would be a train wreck.

Within three weeks she was back, a mere shell of who she had been, her whole being reeking of sorrow. "He wiped the tears from my eyes during the procedure," she said as she wept, "and kept thanking me for doing this for him."

Now her child was gone. And so was he. The train track to healing would be a long one.

CHAPTER 58

One morning, as I drove to the center, I noticed a duck sitting on the side of the grid road as I approached the highway. There were no other ducks in sight, and our weather had already gotten cold enough that the slough beside the road was frozen over. Turning onto the highway, I realized, of course, there was something wrong with the duck, so I turned around and headed back, unsure of my plan.

I stopped the car and slowly got out, trying to assure the duck I would not hurt it. It flapped its wings, one of which was clearly broken. It headed for the frozen water, making valiant efforts to fly without success, and then headed for the reeds on the other side of the slough. I left, knowing it would freeze to death, starve to death, or be killed.

I called Lawrence, sobbing as I related to him what happened. He listened with great empathy and said, "Honey, we both know nature can be cruel."

Why would God lead me to witness this event? A clear analogy formed in my mind of people coming into the center. They look okay on the outside, but are totally broken on the inside. Someone then notices something wrong and offers them help. Then the person goes into "protective mode," instinctively running away from the help, not realizing by running to a place where *they* feel secure, they are heading straight for the trap Satan has set for them.

***

LIFE LESSON #41: *If a broken bone is "set" properly, it becomes stronger at that spot than the rest of the bone. Emotionally and spiritually broken people are the same. Once they allow their brokenness to be healed, they become stronger than others.*

Within three weeks of the previous train wreck, clients came and went, but another one stood out.

What made this appointment bizarre was that it was the boyfriend's mother who made the appointment. What tipped the bizarre scales further was who attended the appointment. I sat there early in the evening with the young woman, her father, her boyfriend, and her boyfriend's mother.

It was another case of a woman at a five on the scale, with tremendous pressure to abort. She'd already had one abortion which caused a lot of grief in her life. It was also clear she had been running from it, but ran straight into the same circumstance. Which may sound odd, but oddly enough, happens a lot. And there was the boyfriend, valiantly trying to explain why she needed to abort.

The thing that made this heartbreaking was the young woman's father. He, too, was pushing her to abort. "If you go ahead and have this kid, you're going to have to figure it out yourself, because you will no longer be living with me." She wept as she listened, unable to look at him as he said the words.

Her mother was not in the picture, and when I asked why, it was evident she was running from some emotional pain. It was not on my agenda to ask what her mother was running from, but her father decided now was the time to reveal to his daughter that her mother had multiple abortions. The look on the young woman's face was one of instant pain.

"Well, now we know what your mom was running from. Thank you for sharing," I said as I looked at him.

"Well what are you going to do?" her father demanded of her.

I urged him to allow *her* to decide; otherwise she could end up resenting him.

"I don't care whether she resents me or not!" he retorted.

The boyfriend's mother also urged him to allow this young couple to decide themselves.

"And where are they going to live?" he asked angrily.

"They can live with me," she responded. She had also had an abortion. As I reviewed what post-abortive grief looked like, and shared my story, you could literally see the ugly puzzle pieces of her life making sense to her.

But it wasn't enough. The young woman's boyfriend already joined forces with her father in an unholy alliance to rid themselves of the child. Finally, the young woman said she had not made up her mind yet, but it was clear another train wreck was now in motion.

I told them I would wait outside the hallway door as they put their coats on. The young woman's father followed me and tried to justify his actions, telling me what a great dad he was. I thanked him for coming in. I prayed as they walked out the door, and I recognized from the conversation that neither the boyfriend nor the young woman's father had anyone to show them how to be a good father.

I never heard from them again.

CHAPTER 59

I found out something interesting before seeing a post-abortive client. Soldiers train to preferably wound and not kill because if someone is wounded, it might take two or three other soldiers out of commission for a period of time because they would tend to the one wounded. They would no longer be engaged in the battle. The light bulb went on. I could see what Satan's tactics are. He wants to wound us, so we will be taken out of the battle.

It also occurred to me Satan would try very hard to eliminate any "officers." In a battle, if you remove the officers—the ones who are giving the orders—the soldiers would be in disarray.

That week, the topic of discussion with a post-abortive woman was avoidance—what we do to avoid anything that reminds us of the trauma we have experienced. We use it as a *defensive* tactic, but what is needed is an *offensive* tactic.

I asked her what she thought soldiers were trained to do, wound or kill? She immediately responded, to kill. Then I told her that they are trained to wound and why.

"You are a Christian, a soldier in God's army," I responded, looking straight into her eyes. "You and I allowed Satan to remove our children, who could have been other soldiers. He also exponentially wounded *us* in the process, so we would be taken out of the battle."

"And others have to tend to the wounds," she said slowly as the revelation made sense. "I want to get back into the battle."

EPILOGUE

It always bothered me when I thought of the vision I had ten years ago while praying, of standing on the edge of a cliff, looking down at Jesus calling to me from a deep, dark abyss, saying "Come and work for me." I wasn't looking up at Him as he spoke to me from the sky, (the typical place you would think to look to see Him). In the vision, I looked down at Him in the darkness.

He is referred to as the God of Abraham, the God of Isaac, and the God of Jacob because He wants to show us He is the same throughout the generations. He has never changed. He will be with you.

The most prevalent instruction in the Bible is to not fear and to not be afraid.

I know many of you are afraid of facing your pain, your darkness. You are in full flight from it. I encourage you to look at your darkness. I promise you will find Him there. Don't allow the evil one to use it against you or your children any longer . . .

God asked me a long time ago if I was willing to face the ugliness of my past so that it could be used for His glory.

Is He asking you?

Will you go?

My people, hear my teaching;
listen to the words of my mouth.
I will open my mouth with a parable;
I will utter hidden things, things from of old—
things we have heard and known,
things our ancestors have told us.
We will not hide them from their descendants;
we will tell the next generation
the praiseworthy deeds of the LORD,
his power, and the wonders He has done.
He decreed statutes for Jacob
and established the law in Israel,
which he commanded our ancestors
to teach their children,
so the next generation would know them,
even the children yet to be born,
and they in turn would tell their children.
Then they would put their trust in God
and would not forget His deeds
but would keep His commands.

PSALM 78:1–7

LIFE LESSON INDEX

LIFE LESSON #9: *If you don't make God the center of your life, Satan will show you other gods to worship.* 30

LIFE LESSON #10: *When you try to avoid emotional pain in your life, you think you are in control of it, but it is controlling you.* 33

LIFE LESSON #11: *"There is a time for everything, and a season for every activity under the heavens." (Ecc. 3:1) You may believe it is the right time for something. But I suggest first asking the One in control of the seasons whether it is your time to bloom.* 35

LIFE LESSON #12: *If you do not think yourself worthy or lovable, you will do unworthy, unlovable things.* 35

LIFE LESSON #13: *As life draws to a close, the things you thought were important, like money, prestige, or power, will not matter. You might have a room, a chest of drawers, and perhaps a shiny new red walker. But what will matter is how you lived your life and what you did with it.* 42

LIFE LESSON #14: *If you do not work through your emotional pain, you may pass it on to future generations without realizing it. Misery loves company.* 50

LIFE LESSON #15: *When we look through the trash of our lives, we will find ugly puzzle pieces that made us who we are. They're smelly and ugly, but until we find them, we will never understand ourselves. And understanding is a huge part of healing.* 59

LIFE LESSON #16: *The truth sets you free.* 60

LIFE LESSON #17: *Mark 11:26 says, "But if you do not forgive, neither will your Father in heaven forgive your transgressions" (NKJV).*

Ouch. I need to pray for those who have hurt me, but if they remain unrepentant, they will inevitably have to answer not to me . . . but to God, the Maker of the Universe.   61

LIFE LESSON #24: If a person has sustained trauma in their life, the body and soul remember the incident and there will be triggers.   84

LIFE LESSON #25: Writing about your feelings, then speaking them aloud are two different things. Writing about your feelings is like lancing a wound. Speaking about them lets the infection drain, relieving the pressure of what can be years of pent up emotion.   87

LIFE LESSON #26: When you start serving the Lord, the evil one will not be happy. Expect and be prepared for pushback.   91

LIFE LESSON #27: You can't help everyone, but if you are obedient you can help those whom the Holy Spirit puts in your path.   99

LIFE LESSON #28: You will not heal if you continue to deny that a wound exists.   101

LIFE LESSON #29: If God moves in a situation, He will do so whether we hold our breath or not. He never asks us to sit and hold our breath. He asks us to pray.   104

LIFE LESSON #30: God's love for us never changes. He loves us the same as yesterday, the same as today, and He will love us the same tomorrow, no matter what has happened.   105

LIFE LESSON #31: You may have had a childhood experience that subconsciously tells you there is not enough to go around, but God has enough love for everyone. And He has enough love for you.   109

LIFE LESSON #39: *People do painful, traumatic things or painful, traumatic things are done to them. Many do not recognize they have God's life jacket on, and they end up in a place of "nothingness," unaware that there is a tab on the life jacket they can pull.*   193

LIFE LESSON #40: *When you see God taking care of the little details in your life, you will be in even more awe when you see Him taking care of the big ones.*   202

LIFE LESSON #41: *If a broken bone is "set" properly, it becomes stronger at that spot than the rest of the bone. Emotionally and spiritually broken people are the same. Once they allow their brokenness to be healed, they become stronger than others.*   213

MEET MELONY MATERI ONLINE

Website: www.melonymateri.com
Blog: www.melonymateri.com/blog
Facebook: www.facebook.com/melonymateri2017

16208524R00126

Made in the USA
Middletown, DE
22 November 2018